COMPREHENSIVE
SECOND EDITION

C INSTRUMENT
EDITION

VOLUME 2
559-877

G-6200IC

7404 South Mason Avenue, Chicago, Illinois 60638

Cover design by Yolanda Durán.

Book design based upon *Worship—Third Edition*
by Michael Tapia.

Published with the approval of the Committee on the Liturgy, United States Conference of Catholic Bishops.

ISBN 1-57999-257-9

1 2 3 4 5 6 7 8 9 10 11 12 13 14 15 16 17 18 19 20

PREFACE

The publication of *Gather Comprehensive—Second Edition* marks the release of GIA's tenth hymnal and service book for Roman Catholic parishes in the United States since the Second Vatican Council. Each of these volumes has had a unique character, and while several have been widely adopted by American parishes, the precursor to this edition, published in 1994, has risen above all the others.

The decision to revise a hymnal is essentially dictated by the church community itself. Increasing inquiries about the possibility of a revision along with a significant drop in adoptions readily signal the time to address the matter. To begin this particular project we incorporated a tool that we hadn't used in a number of years.

A large representative number of parishes who had used *Gather Comprehensive* for an extended period were randomly chosen to receive a detailed and extensive survey. For each item in the original edition, we asked if they had used the item; if not, did they feel that they would use it in the future, and if they felt it should be included in a new edition. The results of this survey became a major factor in choosing the contents for this second edition.

In *Gather Comprehensive—Second Edition* the ritual and service music offerings have been considerably expanded making it even more comprehensive than the original. The established mass settings have been retained, several exciting new settings have been added, and the rites of Christian Initiation, Baptism, Funeral, etc. have been added with appropriate service music. The section of psalms near the beginning of the hymnal retains the most widely sung settings, and in keeping with the spirit of the revised *General Instruction of the Roman Missal* and the document *Liturgiam Authenticam,* all of the lectionary psalm refrains for Sundays and solemnities set by Michel Guimont are now included near the back of the volume.

Like its precursor, this edition includes both contemporary and traditional, or folk-style and classical, or piano/guitar-based and organ-based music—depending on how one chooses to identify musical styles—with the mix leaning toward the former in each case. The accompaniments for many items in the first category are clearly pianistic and cannot effectively be played on the organ without adaptation. To maintain the integrity of performance practice, it is our strong recommendation that these pieces be played on the piano as intended. Other accompaniments, of course, can effectively be played on either organ or piano.

It must be remembered that a hymnal is inherently a book for the gathered assembly. While expanded octavo versions for choir and various instruments exist for many of the titles in this hymnal, hymnal items have been edited to be accessible for the most commonly found resources of assembly with cantor and accompanist.

The introductions to the rites and seasons are by Gabe Huck, taken from *Worship—Third Edition.* Further acknowledgment is hereby given to Jeffry Mickus for project direction, editing, engraving, and book layout; and to Philip Roberts, engraver; Victoria Krstansky and Clarence Reiels, proofreaders; Ronald F. Krisman, Spanish editor; Sarah Parker, survey coordinator; Timothy Redmon, permissions editor; and to all who responded to our survey or supplied detailed recommendations.

Soli Deo gloria.

Alexander Harris
Publisher
Robert J. Batastini
Senior Editor
Kathryn R. Cuddy
Michael A. Cymbala
Kelly Dobbs Mickus
Stephen Petrunak
Editors

INTRODUCTION TO THE INSTRUMENTAL EDITIONS

This edition provides solo instrument accompaniments and descants for most of the hymns, psalms, and songs in *Gather Comprehensive—Second Edition*. Available in two editions, for C and B♭ instruments, it offers the parish instrumentalist an opportunity to lend instrumental enhancement to the assembly song.

Most of the hymns and songs (nos. 323–877) are printed on a system containing multiple staves. The upper staff is the melody, and the second and, where applicable, third staves are harmony and independent parts. For those service music selections that use instruments, a through-composed part is given on a single staff.

Two principal approaches have been used in developing this collection. For classical, organ-based hymns, the instrumental part is most often in the form of a trumpet descant. For piano/guitar-based songs, the instrumental part is most often conceived as woodwind material. All parts, of course, are theoretically playable on any melody instrument, subject to range and technical feasibility. In order to accommodate the range of various instruments, the parts have frequently been printed in octaves.

A typical performance for classical hymns might find the instrument playing the tune along with the organ on the introduction and first stanza, then tacet for a stanza or two, once again playing the tune on a later stanza, and the descant on the final stanza.

For piano/guitar-based selections, the instrumental component is generally more expanded. The melody will be on the top staff, followed by a simple harmony on the second staff and a more independent instrumental part on the third staff. Sometimes the third staff will include parts for two instruments. For a typical performance, the instrument might once again play the melody for the introduction and first refrain or stanza, the simple harmony on inner stanzas, and the more complex part on the final stanza. If more than one instrument is present, the melody and harmony (second staff) generally work very well together as a duet, or the melody might be played by one instrument and the independent part (third staff) by another.

In most cases, the B♭ book is a mere transposition of the C book with octaves adjusted where necessary. Exceptions are the pieces drawn from the Taizé repertoire. For many of these pieces different parts labeled for specific instruments are included in each book.

Above all, remember that this is a resource volume. The final arrangements must be created by the player and the music director. The best arrangement for each piece will be discovered by exploring various options and combinations.

These settings have been drawn from many sources. Where no one is identified as writer of the instrumental part, it can be assumed that it is the work of the original composer or arranger of the piece, or is derived directly from the original keyboard accompaniment. Three GIA editors wrote parts especially for this collection and are identified by their initials: (RJB) Robert J. Batastini, (JM) Jeffry Mickus, and (RS) Randall Sensmeier.

For further reference a bibliography is found at the end of volume 1 which lists additional separately published instrumental parts.

559 Song over the Waters

Tune: Marty Haugen, b.1950, © 1987, GIA Publications, Inc.

560 Lord of All Hopefulness

Tune: SLANE, 10 11 11 12; Gaelic; harm. by Erik Routley, 1917-1982, © 1975, Hope Publishing Co.
Descant: Richard Proulx, b.1937, © 1979, GIA Publications, Inc.

561 Turn My Heart, O God

Tune: Marty Haugen, b.1950, © 2002, GIA Publications, Inc.

563 How Shall We Name God?

Tune: BIRINUS, 7 7 7 7 D; Paul Inwood, b.1947, © 2003, GIA Publications, Inc.

564 Healing River

*The assembly echoes each phrase of the cantor at the interval of one half measure.

2.
Verse 3
D.C.

565 Increase Our Faith

Simple Melody
Last time
Flute Duo
Oboe

568 Ubi Caritas

Tune: Carol E. Browning, b.1956, © 1998, GIA Publications, Inc.

Tune: GOD REMEMBERS, 5 6 7 5 6 6 5 8; Marty Haugen, b.1950, © 2003, GIA Publications, Inc.

573 By the Waters of Babylon

Verses (3)

574 God Weeps with Us Who Weep and Mourn

Tune: MOSHIER, CMD; Sally Ann Morris, b.1952, © 1998, GIA Publications, Inc.

Tune: Michael Mahler, b.1981, © 2003, GIA Publications, Inc.

576 Bless the Lord

Tune: ADORO TE DEVOTE, Mode V; adapt. by David Haas, b.1957, © 1997, GIA Publications, Inc. (JM)

Refrain

Tune: Marty Haugen, b.1950, © 1980, GIA Publications, Inc.

579 A Living Faith

Tune: ST. CATHERINE, LM with refrain; Henry F. Hemy, 1818-1888; adapt. by James G. Walton, 1821-1905
Descant: Hal Hopson, b.1933, © 1979, GIA Publications, Inc.

Refrain
First time only
To verses
Last time
Verses 1-3
D.S.
Verse 4
D.S.

This page has been intentionally left blank.

Tune: Donna Peña, b.1955; arr. by Marty Haugen, b.1950, © 1989, GIA Publications, Inc.

582 Dwelling Place

Tune: John Foley, SJ, b.1939, © 1976 by John B. Foley, SJ, and OCP Publications

583 We Walk by Faith

(5 stanzas)

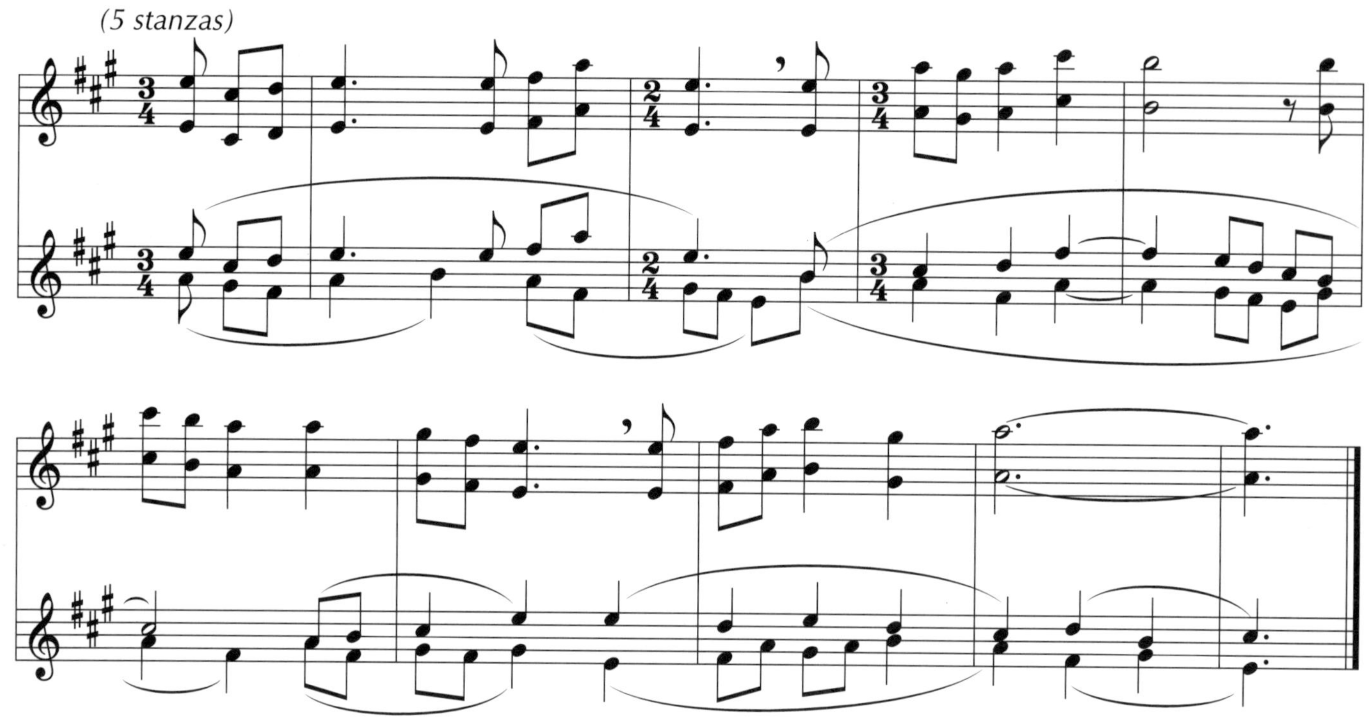

Tune: SHANTI, CM; Marty Haugen, b.1950, © 1984, GIA Publications, Inc.

584 All Will Be Well

Ostinato Refrain

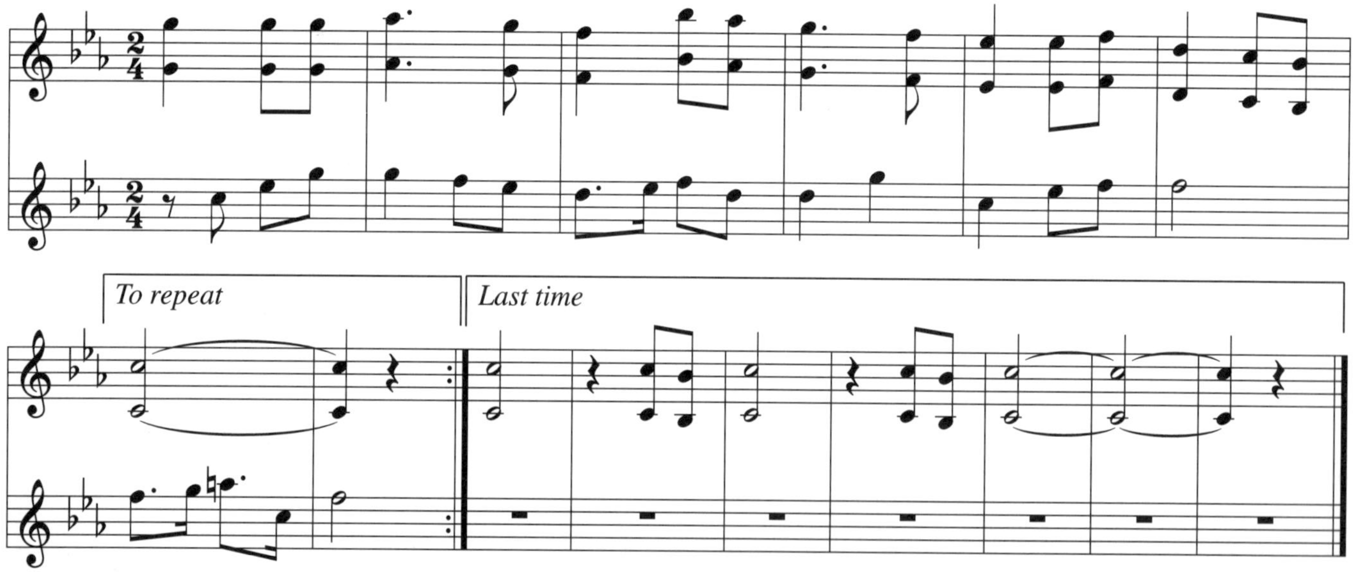

To repeat
Last time

Verses 1, 3, 5

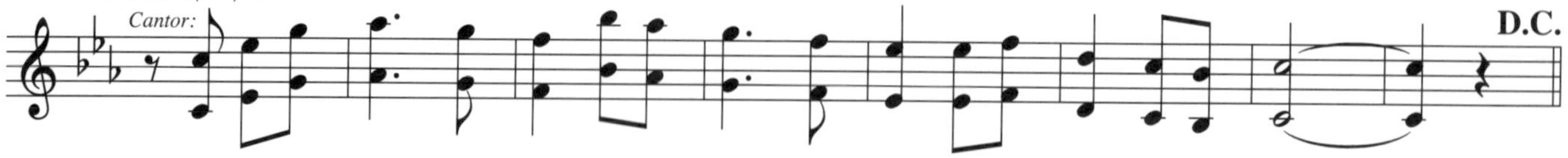

Cantor:
D.C.

Verses 2, 4, 6

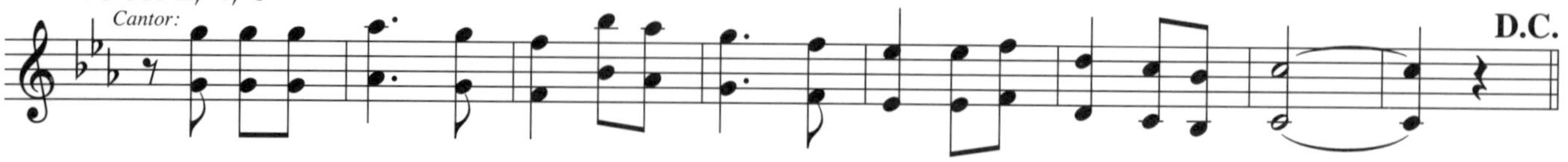

Cantor:
D.C.

Tune: Steven C. Warner, b.1954, © 1993, World Library Publications

Tune: Dan Schutte, b.1947; arr. by Sr. Theophane Hytrek, OSF, 1915-1992;

586 Amazing Grace

Tune: NEW BRITAIN, CM; *Virginia Harmony,* 1831; acc. by Diana Kodner, b.1957, (JM)

Tune: FOUNDATION, 11 11 11 11; Funk's *Compilation of Genuine Church Music,* 1832; harm. by Richard Proulx, b.1937, © 1975, GIA Publications, Inc.
Descant: Richard Proulx, b.1937, © 1997, GIA Publications, Inc.

O God, Our Help in Ages Past 588

Tune: ST. ANNE, CM; attr. to William Croft, 1678-1727; harm. composite from 18th C. versions
Descant: Michael Young, b.1939, © 1979, GIA Publications, Inc.

589 Psalm of Hope

Tune: PSALM OF HOPE, Irregular with refrain; Felix Goebel-Komala, b.1961, © 1994, GIA Publications, Inc. (JM)

Tune: Dan Schutte, b.1947; acc. by Sr. Theophane Hytrek, OSF, 1915-1992, © 1971, Daniel L. Schutte
Instrument part: Randall DeBruyn, © 1992, OCP Publications
Published by OCP Publications.

591 Only in God

D.C.

592 The Lord Is My Light

Tune: Lillian Bouknight; arr. by Paul Gainer, © 1980, Savgos Music, Inc.

593 On Eagle's Wings

Tune: Michael Joncas, b.1951, © 1979, OCP Publications

594 A Mighty Fortress Is Our God

Tune: EIN' FESTE BURG, 8 7 8 7 66 66 7; Martin Luther, 1483-1546; harm. by J.S. Bach, 1685-1750

Tune: Dan Schutte, b.1947; acc. by Michael Pope, SJ, © 1975, Daniel L. Schutte and OCP Publications
Instrument part: Robert J. Dufford, SJ, b.1943, © 1992, Robert J. Dufford, SJ

596 Be Not Afraid

Verse 2
D.S.
Verse 3
D.S.

597 All That We Have

Tune: HOW CAN I KEEP FROM SINGING, 8 7 8 7 with refrain; Robert Lowry, 1826-1899; harm. by Robert J. Batastini, b.1942, © 1988, GIA Publications, Inc. (RJB)

599 The Lord Is Near

*The refrain may be played in a two-part canon at a distance of one measure, or a three-part canon at a distance of one-half measure.

Tune: Michael Joncas, b.1951, © 1979, OCP Publications

600 Seek Ye First

*May be played as a two-part canon.

Tune: VENI CREATOR SPIRITUS, LM; Mode VIII; setting by Richard J. Wojcik, b.1923, © 1975, GIA Publications, Inc. (RS)

Tune: IN BABILONE, 8 7 8 7 D; *Oude en Nieuwe Hollanste Boerenlities,* c.1710
Descant: Robert J. Powell, b.1932, © 1991, GIA Publications, Inc.

604 The Call Is Clear and Simple

Tune: PASSION CHORALE, 7 6 7 6 D; Hans Leo Hassler, 1564-1612; harm. by J. S. Bach, 1685-1750 (RS)

605 Neither Death nor Life

Last time
Last time
Verses 1-4
D.C.
Verses 5, 6
D.C.

1.
D.C.
2.

607 No Greater Love

Tune: Michael Joncas, b. 1951, © 1988, GIA Publications, Inc.

Refrain
1.
2. To verses
Last time
Verse 1
D.C.
Verses 2-4
D.C.

609 Faith, Hope and Love

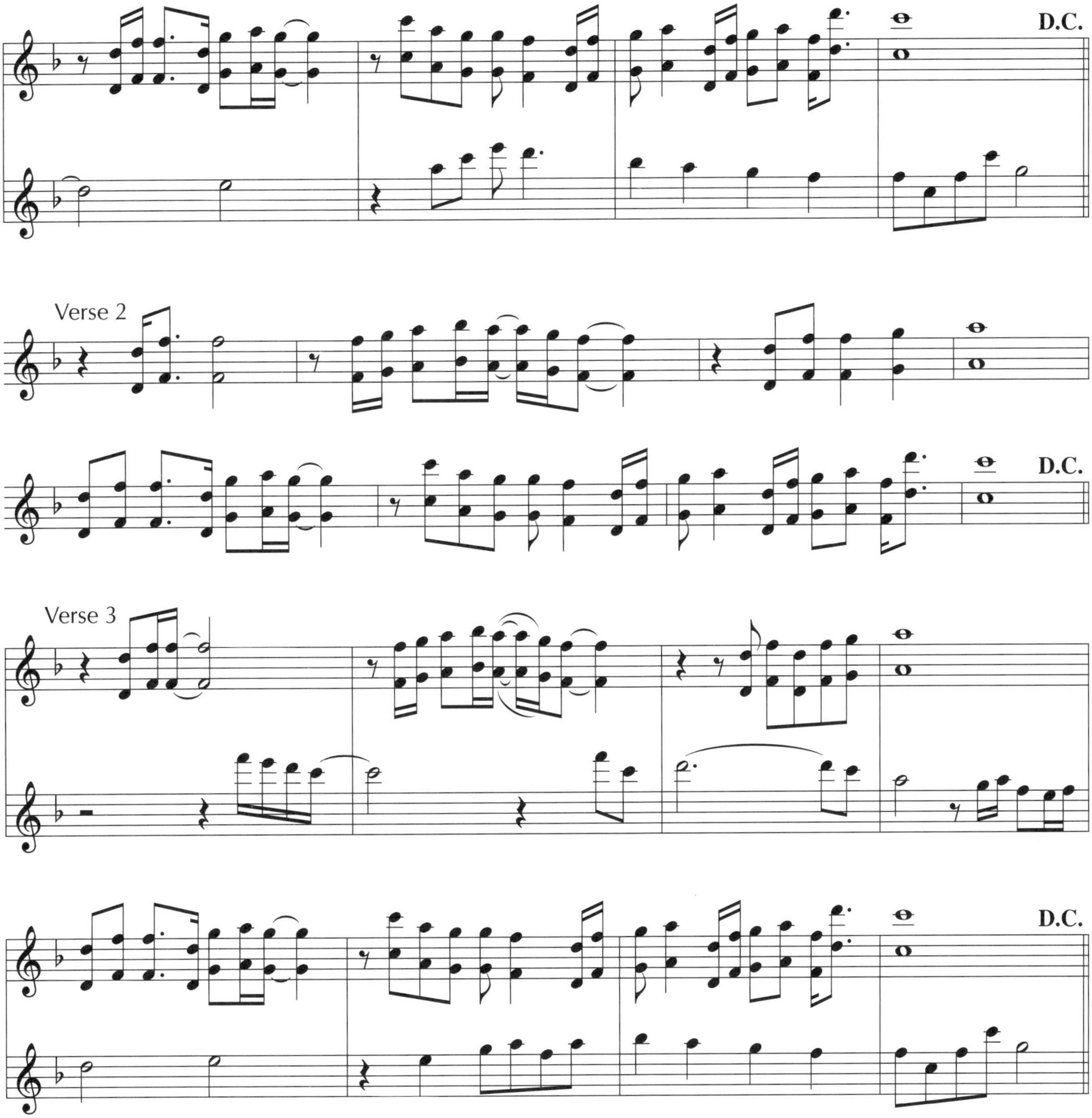
D.C.
Verse 2
D.C.
Verse 3
D.C.

Tune: Francis Patrick O'Brien, b.1958, © 2001, GIA Publications, Inc.

Where Charity and Love Prevail 610

(6 stanzas)

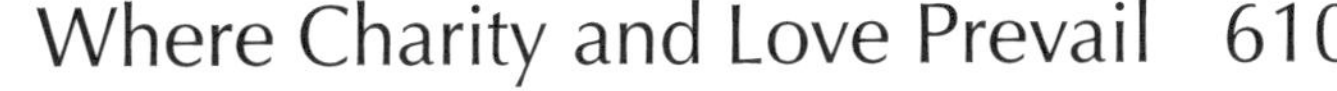

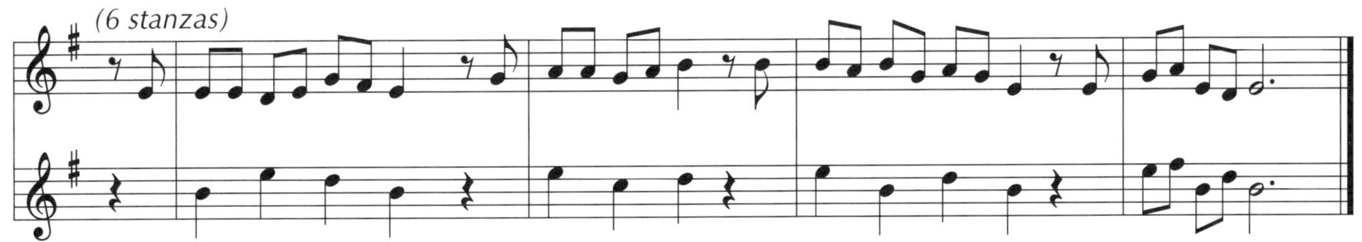

Tune: CHRISTIAN LOVE, CM; Paul Benoit, OSB, 1893-1979, © 1960, 1961, World Library Publications (RS)

611 Set Your Heart on the Higher Gifts

Tune: Steven C. Warner, b.1954, © 1992, 1994, World Library Publications

Tune: COMFORT, 8 7 8 7 with refrain; Michael Joncas, b.1951, © 1988, GIA Publications, Inc.

613 Love Divine, All Loves Excelling

Tune: HYFRYDOL, 8 7 8 7 D; Rowland H. Prichard, 1811-1887 (RS)

Tune: WONDEROUS LOVE, 12 9 12 12 9; *Southern Harmony,* 1835, harm. from *Cantate Domino, 1980,*

615 My Song Will Be for You Forever

Refrain

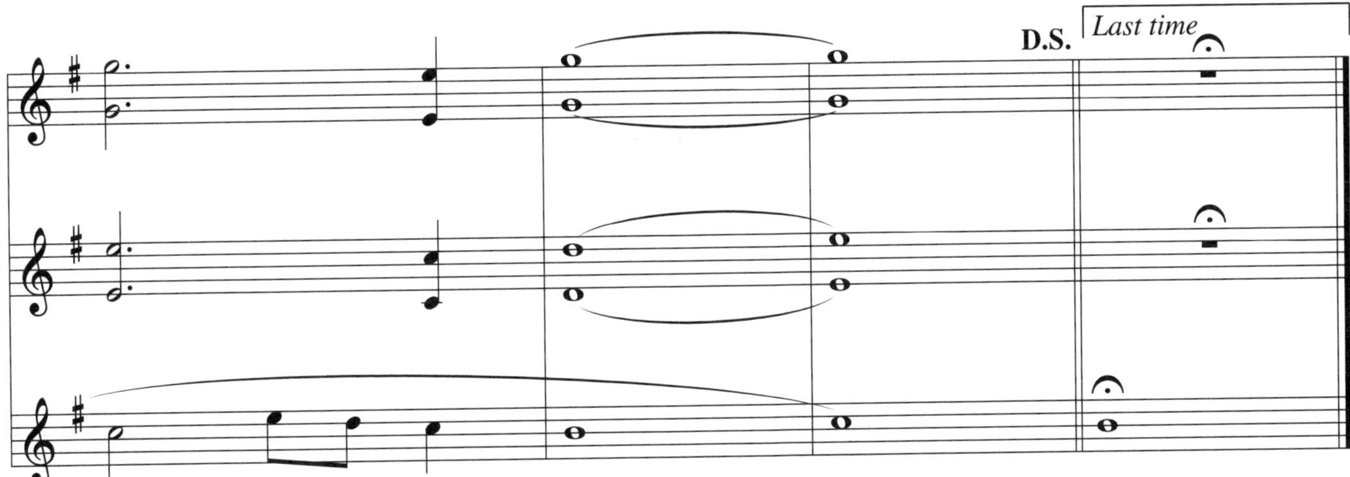
D.S.
Last time

616 Eye Has Not Seen

Verses (4)
1.-3.
D.C.
4.
D.C.

This page has been intentionally left blank.

Tune: BALM IN GILEAD, Irregular; African-American spiritual; acc. by Marty Haugen, b.1950, © 2003, GIA Publications, Inc. (RJB)

619 The Clouds' Veil

Tune: Liam Lawton, b.1959; arr. by John McCann, b.1961, © 1997, GIA Publications, Inc.

620 Our God Is Rich in Love

D.C.
Verse 2
D.C.
Verse 3
D.C.

621 The Lord Will Heal the Broken Heart

Tune: Liam Lawton, b.1959; arr. John McCann, b.1961, © 2000, GIA Publications, Inc.

Tune: KINGSFOLD, CMD; English; harm. by Ralph Vaughan Williams, 1872-1958, © Oxford University Press
Descant: Richard Proulx, b.1937, © 1979, GIA Publications, Inc.

623 With You by My Side

Tune: David Haas, b.1957, © 1998, GIA Publications, Inc.

624 Shepherd of My Heart

Tune: Francis Patrick O'Brien, b.1958, © 1992, GIA Publications, Inc.

626 Nada Te Turbe / Nothing Can Trouble

Tune: Jacques Berthier, 1923-1994,

627 You Are Mine

Tune: David Haas, b.1957, © 1991, GIA Publications, Inc.

Tune: James J. Chepponis, b.1956, © 1992, GIA Publications, Inc.

630 Come to Me, O Weary Traveler

(4 stanzas)

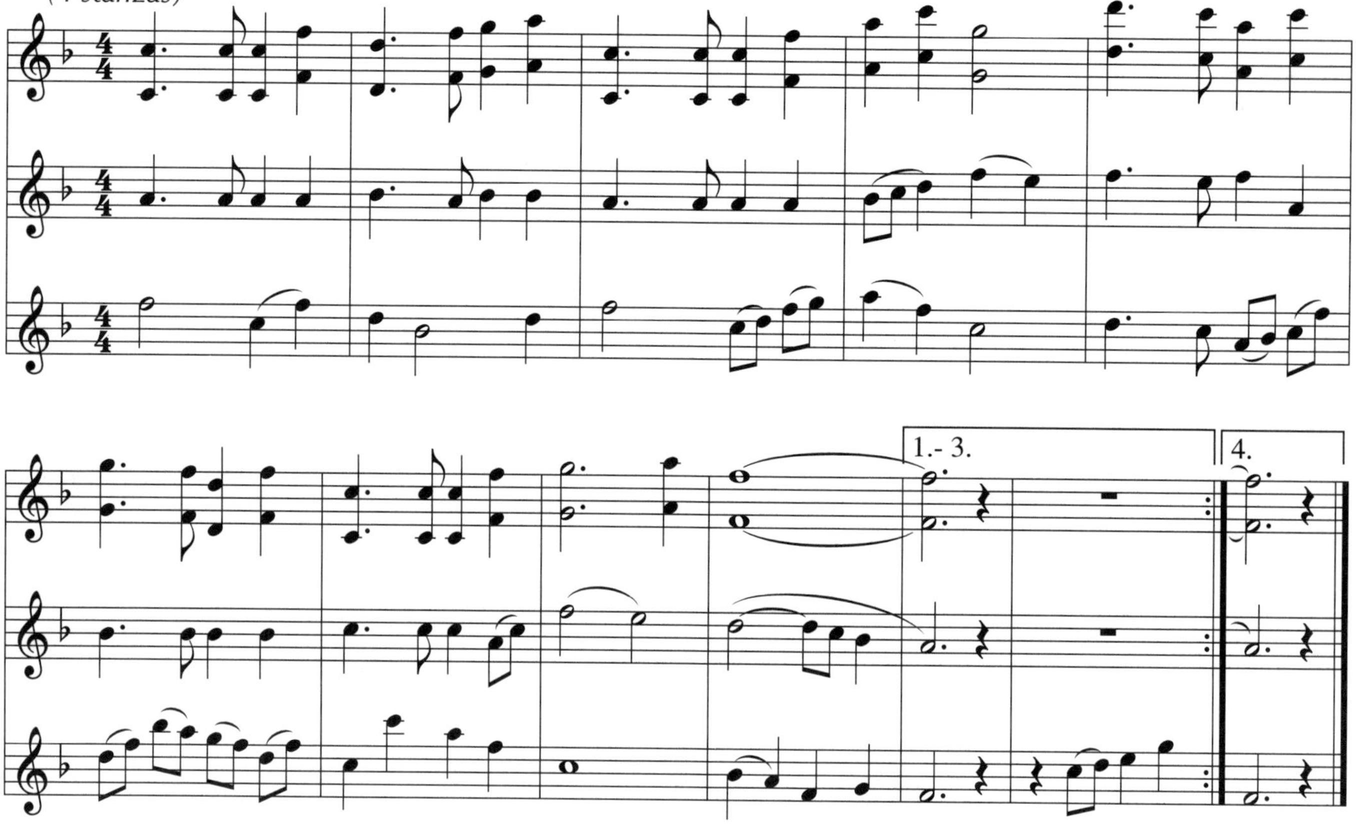

1.- 3.

4.

Tune: DUNSTAN, 8 7 8 7; Bob Moore, b.1962, © 1993, GIA Publications, Inc.

631 The King of Love My Shepherd Is

Tune: ST. COLUMBA, 8 7 8 7; Gaelic; harm. by A. Gregory Murray, OSB, 1905-1992, © Downside Abbey
Descant: John Ferguson, b.1941, © 1992, GIA Publications, Inc.

Jesus, Lead the Way 632

Tune: ROCHELLE, 55 88 55; Adam Drese, 1620-1701; harm. alt. (RS)

633 Come to Me

Verse 3
D.C.

634 Shelter Me, O God

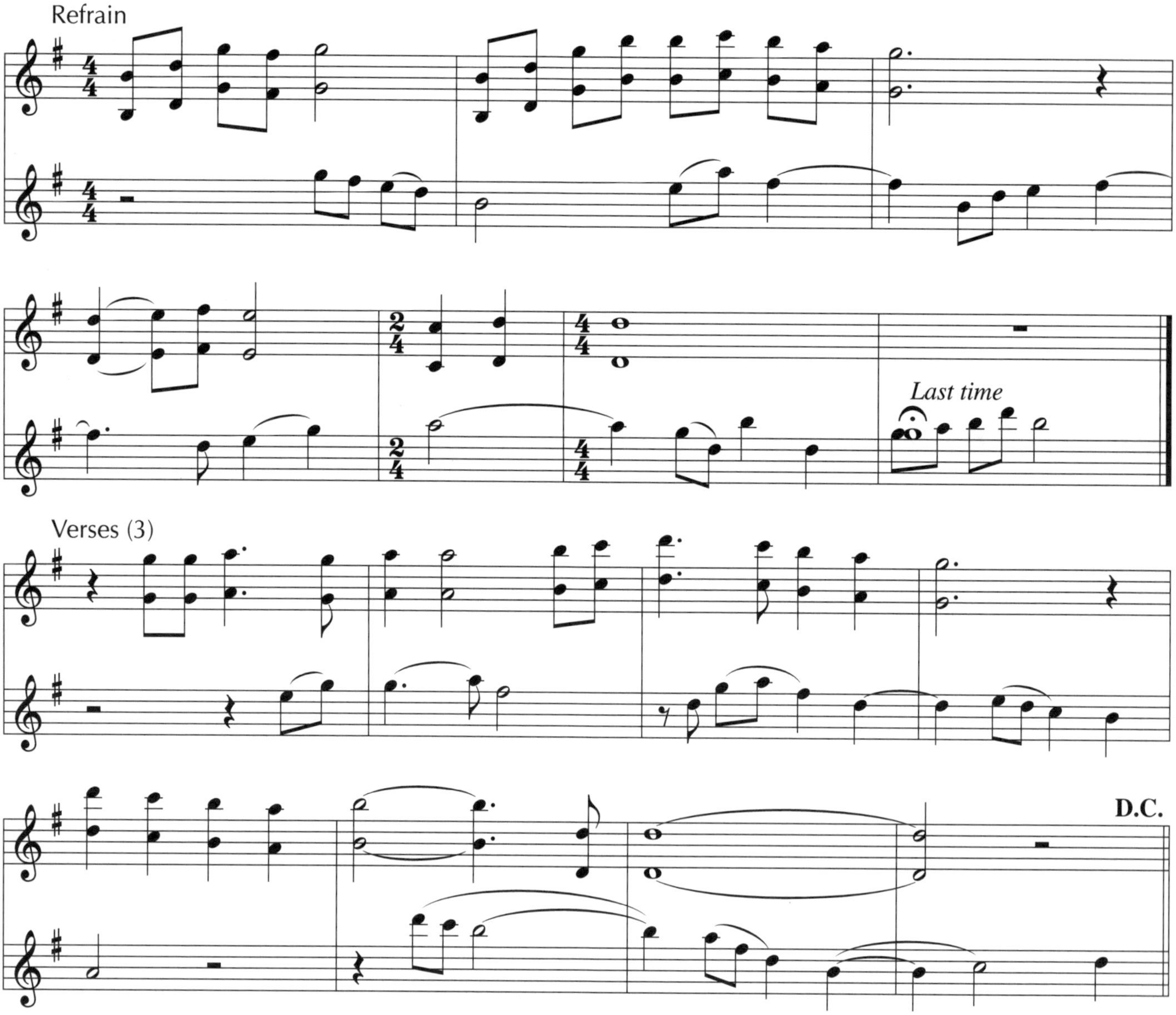
Refrain
Last time
Verses (3)
D.C.

Tune: Bob Hurd, b.1950, © 1984, Bob Hurd; harm. by Craig S. Kingsbury, b.1952, © 1984, OCP Publications
Published by OCP Publications.

635 Blest Are They

Verses 1-3
4
4

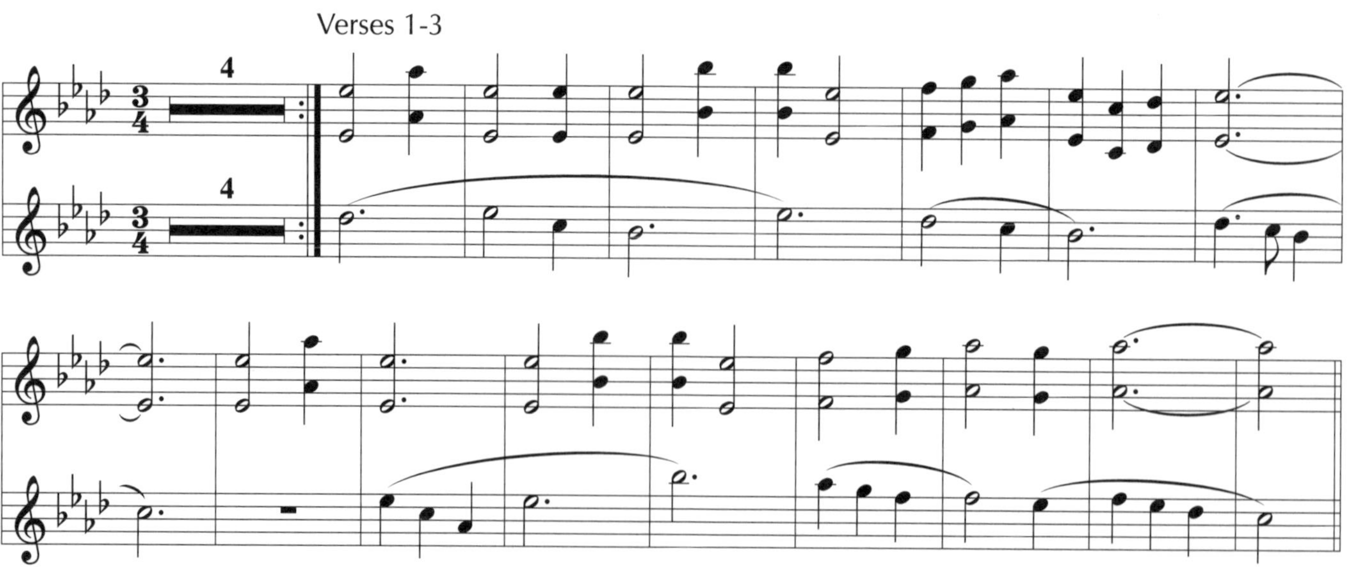

Refrain
1.- 4.
To verses
Last time
Verses 4, 5
D.S.

637 The Kingdom of God

Oboe
I
3
3
3
II
3
3

638 Within the Reign of God

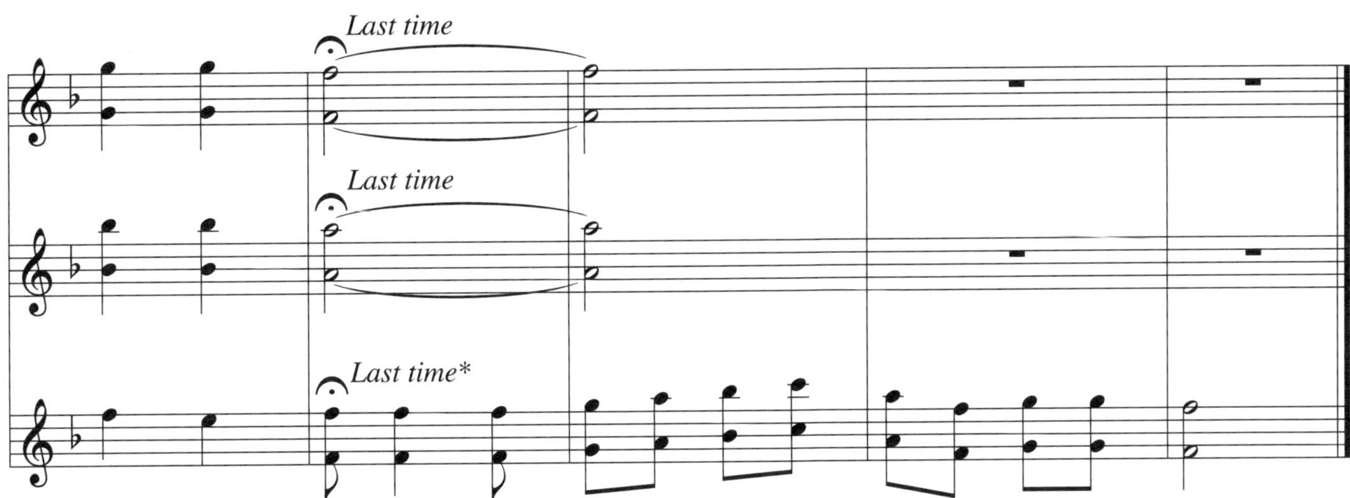

*Last four bars may be played in between verses and/or as a solo at the end of the piece (as others are holding fermata.)

Tune: Marty Haugen, b.1950, © 1999, GIA Publications, Inc.

The Kingdom of God 639

Tune: LAUDATE DOMINUM, 10 10 11 11; Charles H. H. Parry, 1840-1918
Descant: Eugene Englert, b.1931, © 1980, GIA Publications, Inc.

640 Bring Forth the Kingdom

Tune: Marty Haugen, b.1950, © 1986, GIA Publications, Inc.

Tune: McKEE, CM; African-American; adapt. by Harry T. Burleigh, 1866-1949
Descant: Richard Proulx, b.1937, © 1979, GIA Publications, Inc.

Christ Is Made the Sure Foundation 642

Tune: ST. THOMAS, 8 7 8 7 8 7; John F. Wade, 1711-1786 (RS)

643 As a Fire Is Meant for Burning

Tune: BEACH SPRING, 8 7 8 7 D; *The Sacred Harp,* 1844; harm. by Marty Haugen, b.1950, © 1985, GIA Publications, Inc.

Sing a New Church 644

Tune: NETTLETON, 8 7 8 7 D; Wyeth's *Repository of Sacred Music, Pt. II,* 1813
Descant: Austin C. Lovelace, b.1919, © 1992, GIA Publications, Inc.

O Christ the Great Foundation 646

(4 stanzas)

Tune: AURELIA, 7 6 7 6 D; Samuel S. Wesley, 1810-1876
Descant: Harold Owen, b.1931, © 1979, GIA Publications, Inc.

647 Where Your Treasure Is

*Play top note when going into Vs. 4.

Tune: Marty Haugen, b.1950, © 2000, GIA Publications, Inc.

648 Jesus, Your Spirit in Us

(4 English stanzas, 4 Spanish verses)

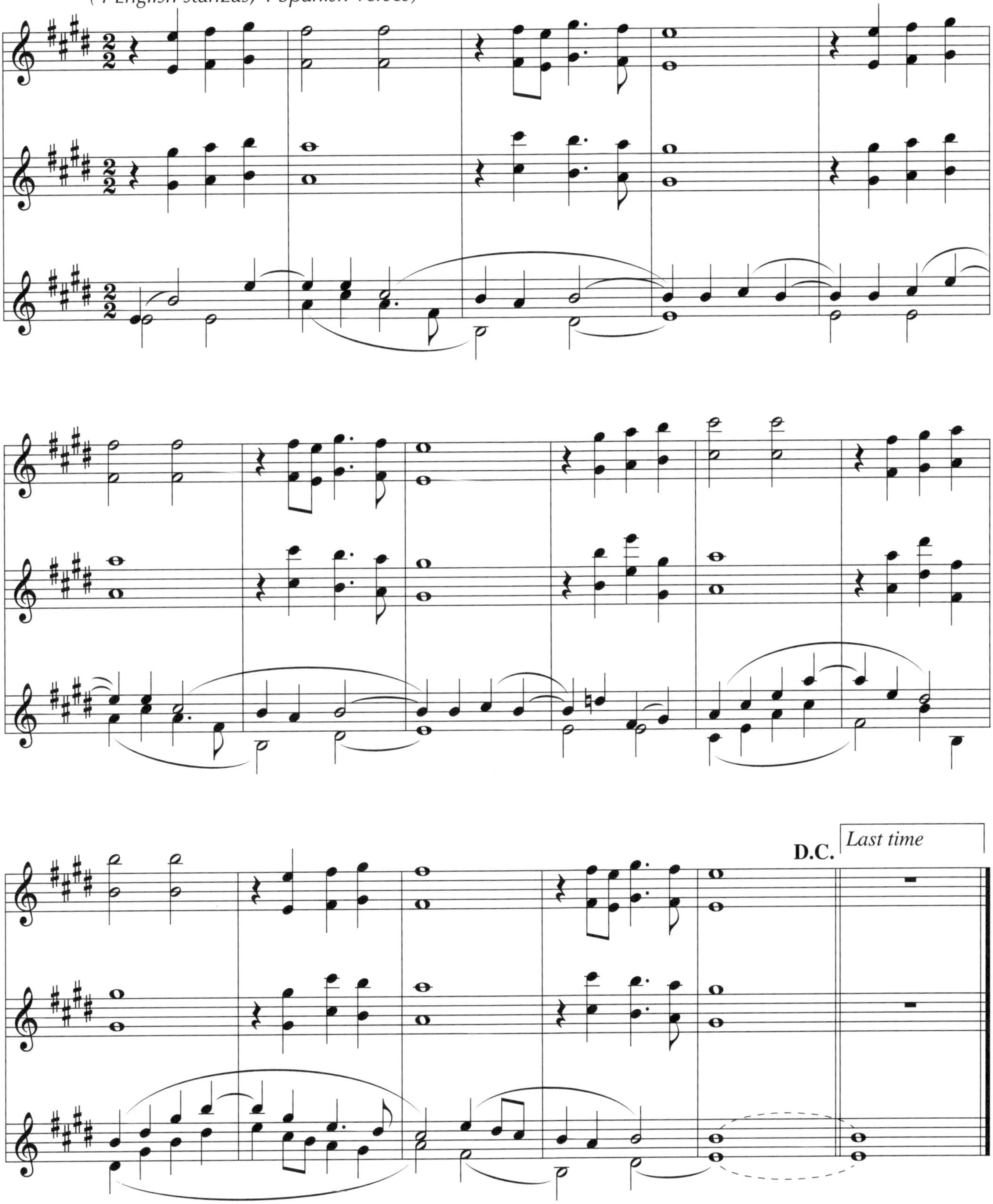

D.C. *Last time*

Tune: SOMOS DEL SEÑOR, Irregular; arr. by Ronald F. Krisman, b.1946,

652 We Will Serve the Lord

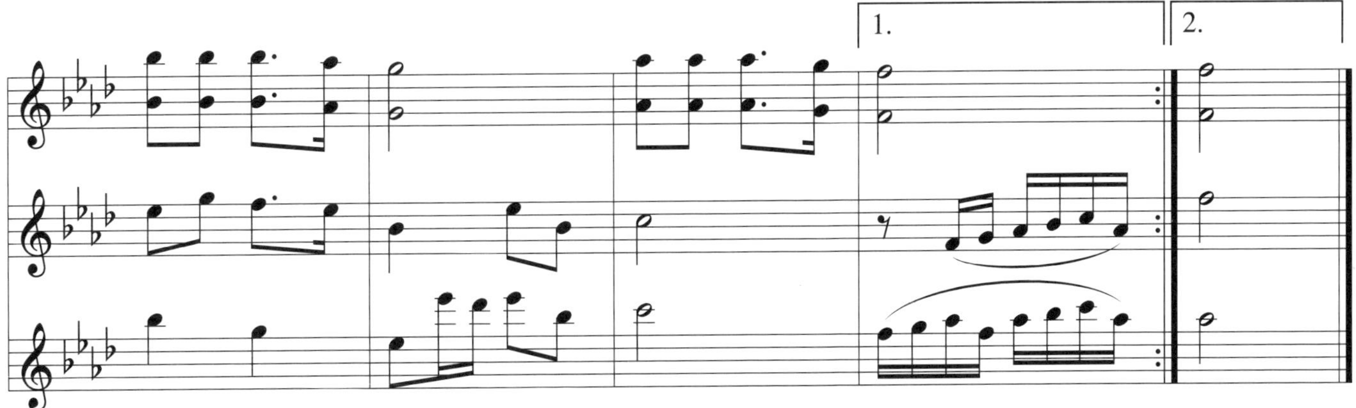

Tune: Rory Cooney, b.1952, © 1986, North American Liturgy Resources. Published by OCP Publications.

All That Is Hidden 654

Verses (4)

Refrain

Last time

Last time

Tune: Bernadette Farrell, b.1957, © 1986, 1988, Bernadette Farrell. Published by OCP Publications.

655 Take This Moment

(5 stanzas)

Last time

Tune: TAKE THIS MOMENT, 7 5 7 5; John L. Bell, b.1949, © 1989, Iona Community, GIA Publications, Inc., agent

656 Whatsoever You Do

Refrain

Verses (11)

D.C.

Tune: WHATSOEVER YOU DO, 10 10 11 with refrain; Willard F. Jabusch, b.1930, © 1966, 1982; harm. by Robert J. Batastini, b.1942
Administered by OCP Publications.

'Tis the Gift to Be Simple 657

Tune: SIMPLE GIFTS; arr. Margaret W. Mealy, b.1922, © 1984 (JM)

658 Keep in Mind

Refrain

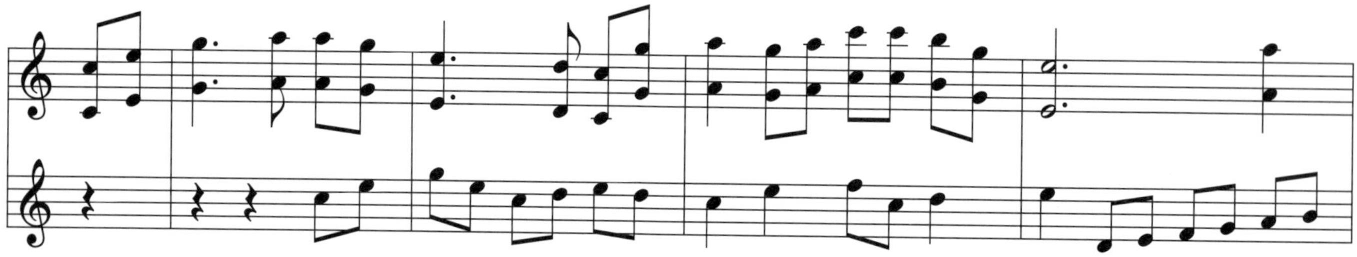

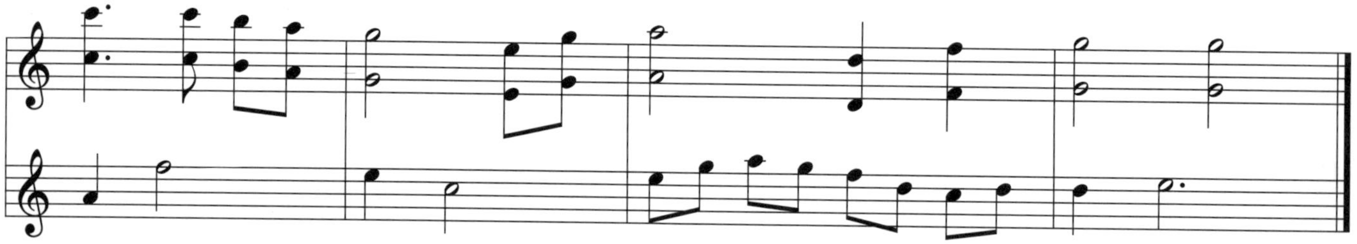

Verse 1

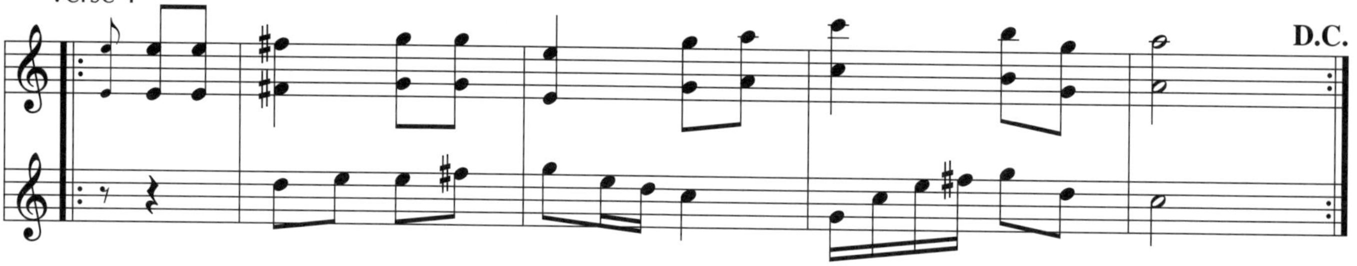

D.C.

Verses 2, 3

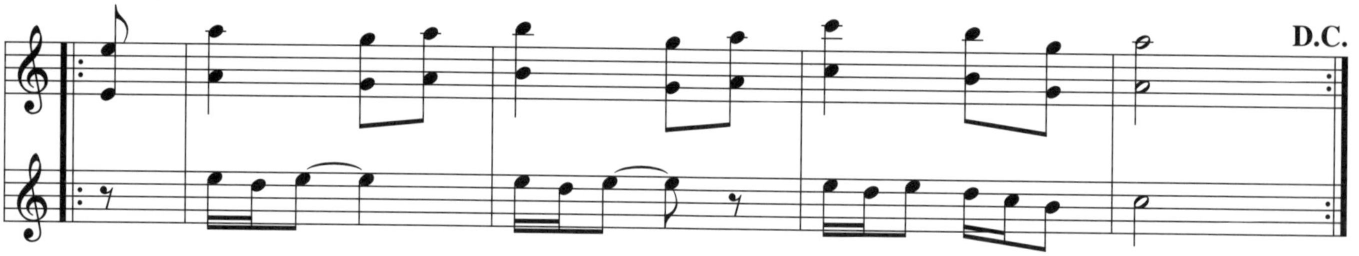

D.C.

Tune: Lucien Deiss, CSSp, b.1921, © 1965, 1966, World Library Publications
Descant: Kevin Keil, b.1956, © 1996, GIA Publications, Inc.

659 Jesus in the Morning

Tune: African-American folk song

Deliver Us, O Lord of Truth 660

Tune: LAND OF REST, CM; American; harm. by Annabel M. Buchanan, 1888-1983, © 1938, 1966, J. Fisher and Bro. (RS)

The Servant Song 661

Tune: Richard Gillard, b.1953, harm. by Betty Pulkingham, b.1929, © 1977, Scripture in Song (RS)

662 You Have Anointed Me

Tune: Mike Balhoff, b.1946, Gary Daigle, b.1957, Darryl Ducote, b.1945; acc. by Gary Daigle, b.1957, © 1981, Damean Music. Distributed by GIA Publications, Inc.

663 City of God

Refrain
1.
2. To verse 3
3. To verse 4
4.

Verse 3
(Verse 4)
To refrain

(5 stanzas)

666 Go Make of All Disciples

Tune: ELLACOMBE, 7 6 7 6 D; *Gesangbuch der Herzogl,* Wirtemberg, 1784
Descant: Robert J. Powell, b.1932, © 1991, GIA Publications, Inc.

Tune: IN BABILONE, 8 7 8 7 D; *Oude en Nieuwe Hollanste Boerenlities,* c.1710
Descant: Robert J. Powell, b.1932, © 1991, GIA Publications, Inc.

669 God Has Chosen Me

Tune: Bernadette Farrell, b.1957, © 1990, Bernadette Farrell. Published by OCP Publications.

*May be played as a canon.

671 Here I Am, Lord

Tune: Dan Schutte, b.1947; arr. by Michael Pope, SJ, and John Weissrock, © 1981, OCP Publications (RJB)

Thuma Mina / Send Me, Jesus 674

Tune: THUMA MINA, South African, © 1984, Utryck, Walton Music Corp., agent

You Are Called to Tell the Story 675

(4 stanzas)

Tune: ROSEMARY, 8 7 8 7 8 7; Marty Haugen, b.1950, © 2002, GIA Publications, Inc.

676 I Am for You

Tune: Rory Cooney, b.1952, © 1993, GIA Publications, Inc.

Verses (2)

Refrain

1., 3.
Final ending
2.
D.S.

Lord, When You Came / Pescador de Hombres

Tune: Cesáreo Gabaráin, © 1979, published by OCP Publications; acc. by Diana Kodner, b.1957 (JM)

679 You Walk along Our Shoreline

Tune: AURELIA, 7 6 7 6 D; Samuel S. Wesley, 1810-1876
Descant: Harold Owen, b.1931, © 1979, GIA Publications, Inc.

680 The Love of the Lord

1., 3.
2., 4.
Refrain
Last time D.C.

681 Anthem

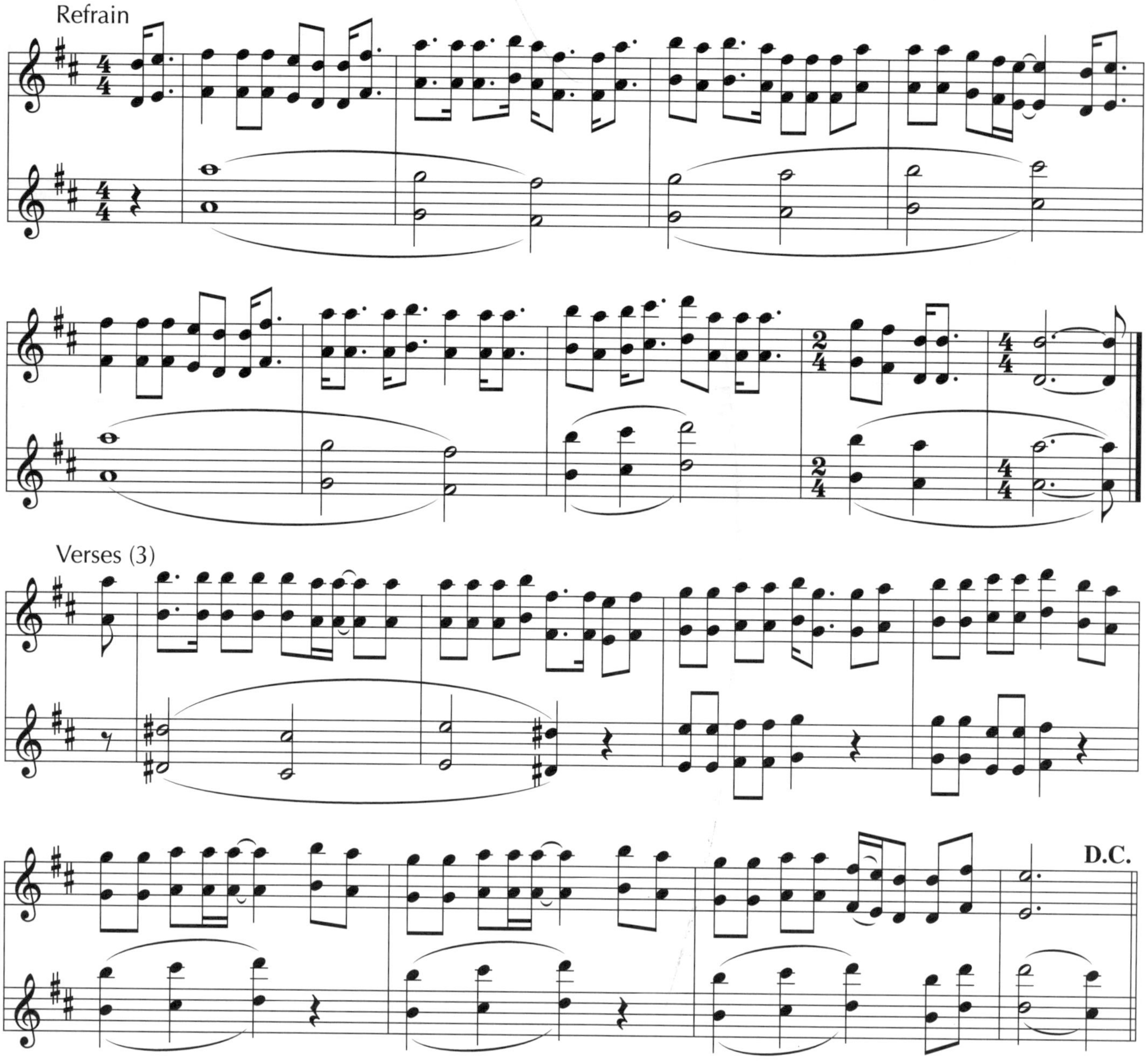
Refrain
Verses (3)
D.C.

Tune: Tom Conry, b.1951, © 1978, OCP Publications; acc. by Robert J. Batastini, b.1942

682 Blest Are We / Bendecidos, Somos Santos

Refrain

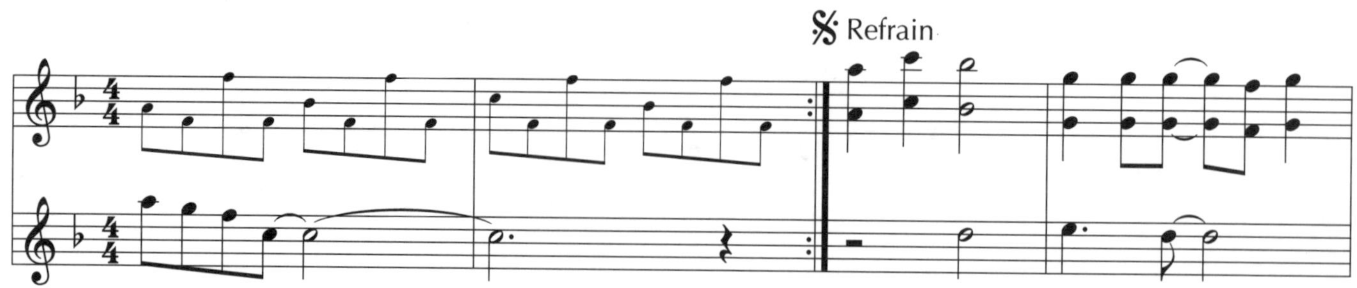

*Last time, repeat final 4 bars.

685 Song of St. Patrick

Verses 2-5

Tune: Marty Haugen, b.1950, © 1986, GIA Publications, Inc.

686 Come and Journey with a Savior

Tune: COME AND JOURNEY, 8 7 8 7 with refrain; Marty Haugen, b.1950, © 1998, GIA Publications, Inc.

Tune: KELVINGROVE, 7 6 7 6 777 6; Scottish traditional; arr. by John L. Bell, b.1949,

688 Take Up Your Cross

D.C.
Verse 2
D.C.

689 I Danced in the Morning

*Cues for vss. 2–5

Tune: LORD OF THE DANCE, Irregular; adapted from a traditional Shaker melody by Sydney Carter, 1915-2004, © 1963, Stainer & Bell, Ltd., London, England. (admin. by Hope Publishing Co.)

Tune: O WALY WALY, LM; English; harm. by Martin West, b.1929, © 1983, Hope Publishing Co.
Descant: Robert A. Hobby, © 1992, GIA Publications, Inc.

691 Give the Lord Your Heart

Tune: Michael Mahler, b.1981
Solo part: Jim Gailloreto

692 Take, O Take Me As I Am

Tune: John L. Bell, b.1949, © 1995, Iona Community, GIA Publications, Inc., agent

Tune: LEAVE ALL THINGS, CMD with refrain; Suzanne Toolan, SM, b.1927,

694 We Have Been Told

Tune: David Haas, b.1957, © 1983, GIA Publications, Inc.

695 Here Am I, Lord

Tune: Timothy Valentine, SJ, b.1959, © 1998, GIA Publications, Inc. (RJB)

696 Now We Remain

(vs. 2, 3)
(vs. 2, 3)
1.- 3.
4.
D.C.
D.C.

697 Sing Yes for the Carpenter

Tune: ROCKY POINT, 9 7 9 7 with refrain; Rob Glover, b.1950, © 1997, GIA Publications, Inc.

699 Unless a Grain of Wheat

Tune: Bernadette Farrell, b.1957, © 1983, Bernadette Farrell. Published by OCP Publications.

Verses (3)

Refrain

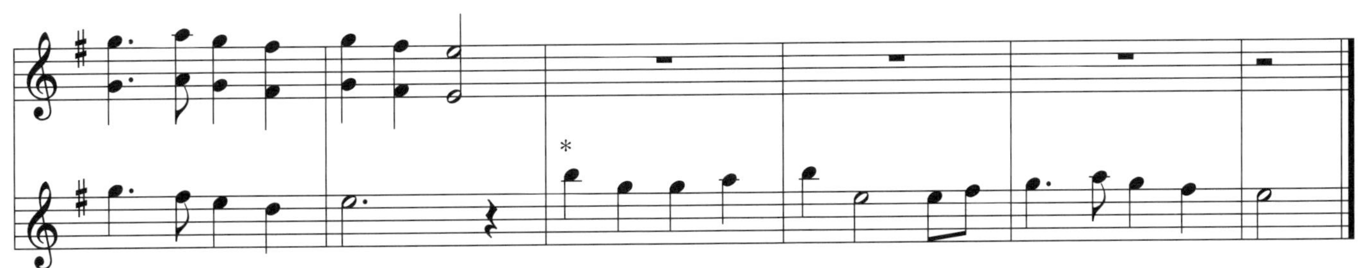

*This may be used as an introduction.

Tune: JUSTICE, 8 6 8 7 with refrain; Paul A. Tate, b.1968,

701 Only This I Want

Tune: Dan Schutte, b.1947; arr. by Michael Pope, SJ, © 1981, Daniel L. Schutte and OCP Publications (JM)

Refrain
Last time
Last time
Verses 1, 2
All:
Cantor:
1., 2., 4., 5.
3., 6.
D.C.
Verse 3
All:
Cantor:
1.- 6.
7.
D.C.

703 Abundant Life

Tune: LA GRANGE, 8 7 8 7 D; Marty Haugen, b.1950, © 1994, GIA Publications, Inc.

Tune: HYMN TO JOY, 8 7 8 7 D; arr. from Ludwig van Beethoven, 1770-1827, by Edward Hodges, 1796-1867
Descant: Harold Owen, b.1931,

705 A Place at the Table

Tune: Lori True, b.1961
Instrument Part: David Haas, b.1957

706 We Come with Joy

Tune: FOREST GREEN, CMD; English, harm. by Ralph Vaughan Williams, 1872-1958, alt., © Oxford University Press (RS)

Tune: South African, © 1984, Utryck, Walton Music Corporation, agent

708 If You Believe and I Believe

Tune: Zimbabwean traditional; adapt. of English traditional; as taught by Tarasai; arr. by John L. Bell, b.1949,

Refrain
Last time
Last time
Last time

Verse 1
D.C.
Verse 2
D.C.

Verses 3, 4
D.C.
Verse 5
D.C.

710 We Are Called

Refrain
1., 2.
3.

711 We Shall Overcome

Tune: adapt. by Zilphia Horton, Frank Hamilton, Guy Carawan, and Pete Seeger, © 1960, 1963, Ludlow Music; harm. by J. Jefferson Cleveland, b.1937, © 1981, by Abingdon Press

Tune: ST. THOMAS, 8 7 8 7 8 7; John F. Wade, 1711-1786 (RS)

Tune: STANISLAUS, 3 7 6 5 D 3; Daniel Charles Damon, b.1955, © 1995, Hope Publishing Co. (JM)

714 What You Have Done for Me

Tune: Tony E. Alonso, b.1980, © 2001, GIA Publications, Inc.

715 On Holy Ground

1.- 5.
D.C.
Final ending
3

716 The Harvest of Justice

Refrain and Verses (3)

Tune: David Haas, b.1957, © 1985, GIA Publications, Inc.

Tune: PASSION CHORALE, 7 6 7 6 D; Hans Leo Hassler, 1564-1612; harm. by J. S. Bach, 1685-1750 (RS)

Refrain

Tune: Marty Haugen, b.1950, © 1985, GIA Publications, Inc.

719 The Peace of God

Verse 2

Tune: David Haas, b.1957, © 2002, GIA Publications, Inc.

Prayer of Peace 720

(6 stanzas)

Tune: David Haas, b.1957, © 1987, GIA Publications, Inc. (RJB)

721 Make Me a Channel of Your Peace

D.C.

723 Let There Be Peace on Earth

Tune: Sy Miller, 1908-1941, Jill Jackson, b.1913, © 1955, 1983, Jan-Lee Music; acc. by Diana Kodner, b.1957, © 1993, GIA Publications, Inc. Used with permission.

Dona Nobis Pacem 724

Canon

1.

2.

3.

Tune: Traditional; acc. by Diana Kodner, b.1957, © 1994, GIA Publications, Inc.

725 Peace Is Flowing Like a River

Tune: Unknown; acc. by Diana Kodner, b.1957, © 1993, GIA Publications, Inc. (RJB)

Tune: McKEE, CM; African-American; adapt. by Harry T. Burleigh, 1866-1949
Descant: Richard Proulx, b.1937,

727 We Are Many Parts

Tune: Marty Haugen, b.1950, © 1980, 1986, GIA Publications, Inc.

728 They'll Know We Are Christians

Tune: ST. BRENDAN'S, 7 6 7 6 8 6 with refrain; Peter Scholtes, b.1938, © 1966, F.E.L. Publications, assigned to The Lorenz Corp., 1991 (RJB)

Diverse in Culture, Nation, Race 729

**May be played as a two- or four-part canon.*

Tune: TALLIS' CANON, LM; Thomas Tallis, c.1510-1583 (RS)

Jesus Christ, Yesterday, Today and for Ever 730

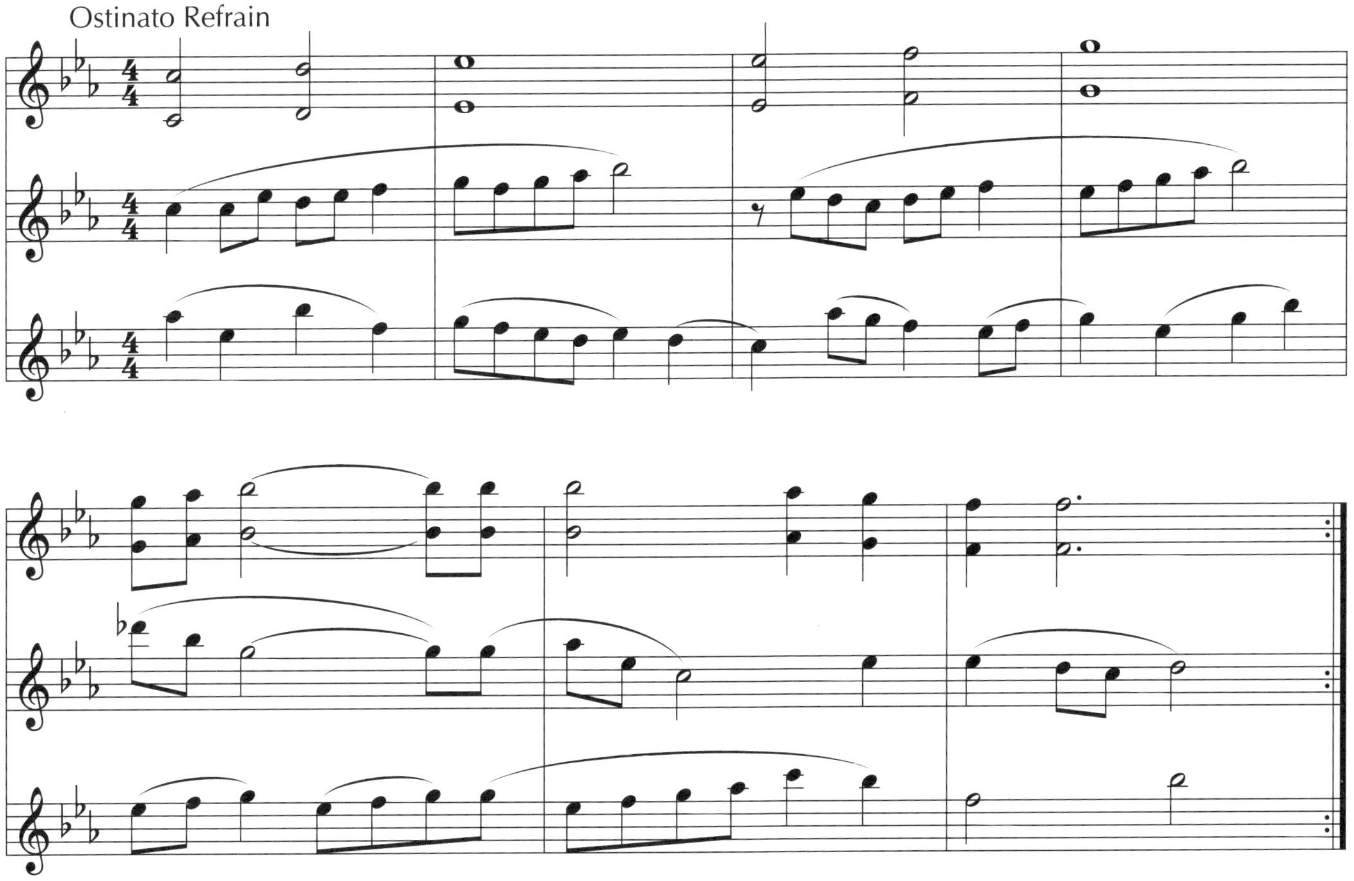

Ostinato Refrain

Tune: Suzanne Toolan, SM, b.1927, © 1988, GIA Publications, Inc. (RJB)

731 Jesus Is the Resurrection

Tune: Derek Campbell, 1963-2004, © 2002, GIA Publications, Inc. (RJB)

Christ Has Promised to Be Present 732

Tune: STUTTGART, 8 7 8 7; *Psalmodia Sacra,* 1715; adapt. and harm. by William Henry Havergal, 1793-1870, alt.
Descant: Harold Owen, b.1931, © 1979, GIA Publications, Inc.

733 Alleluia! Give the Glory

To verses
Last time
Verses (2)
D.C.

Refrain

To verses
Final ending
Verses (3)
D.C.

735 Gather 'Round This Table

Tune: Marty Haugen, b.1950, © 1999, 2001, GIA Publications, Inc.

What Is This Place 736

(3 stanzas)

Tune: KOMT NU MET ZANG, 9 8 9 8 9 66; Valerius' *Neder-landtsche gedenck-klanck;* acc. by Robert J. Batastini, b.1942, © 1987, GIA Publications, Inc.

737 God Is Here! As We His People

Tune: ABBOT'S LEIGH, 8 7 8 7 D; Cyril V. Taylor, 1907-1991, (RS)

Tune: HOLY MANNA, 8 7 8 7 D; William Moore, fl.1830; acc. by Kelly Dobbs Mickus, b.1966,

739 Come, Let Us Sing with Joy to the Lord

Tune: Paul A. Tate, b.1968, © 2001, World Library Publications

740 Come to Us

Tune: TWO OAKS, 9 6 8 6 8 7 10 with refrain; Marty Haugen, b. 1950, © 1994, GIA Publications, Inc.

742 Gather Your People

*Cues for vss. 2–4

Tune: GATHER US IN, Irregular; Marty Haugen, b.1950,

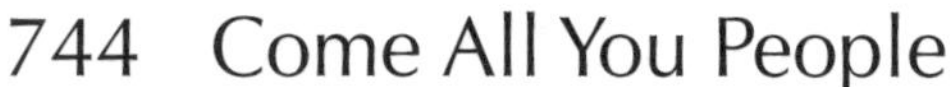

744 Come All You People

3
Last time
Last time
3

Tune: Alexander Gondo; arr. by John L. Bell, b.1949, © 1994, The Iona Community, GIA Publications, Inc., agent

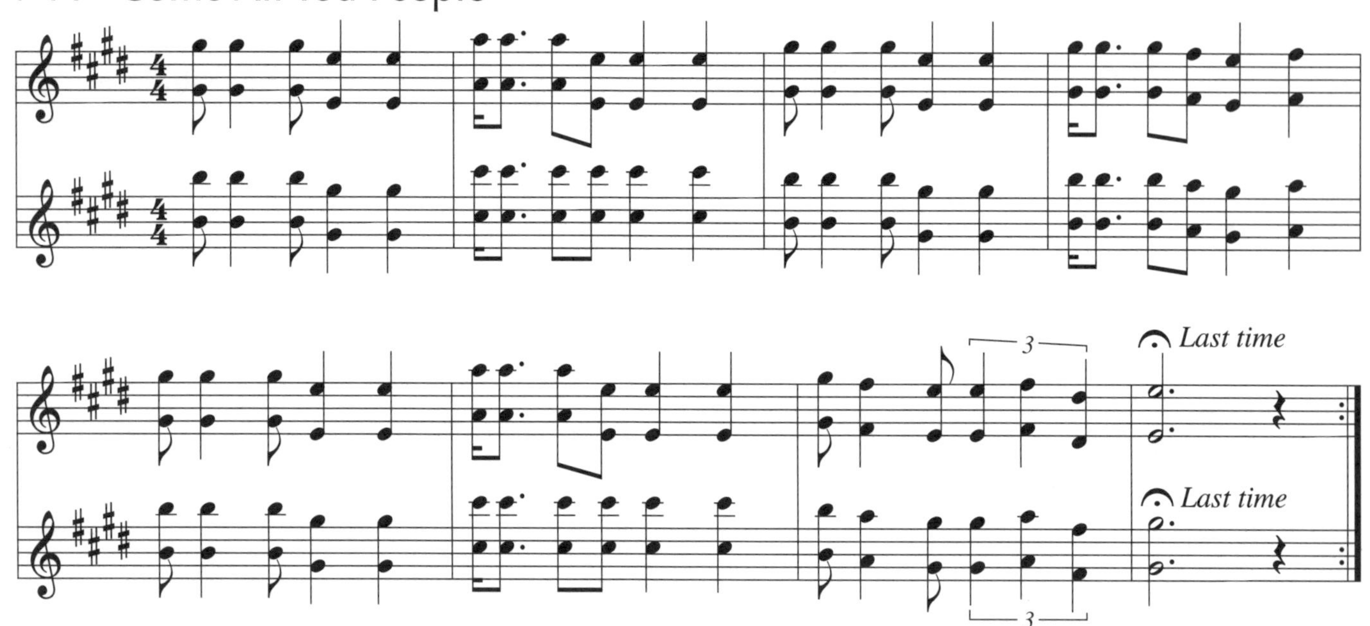

745 Gathered as One

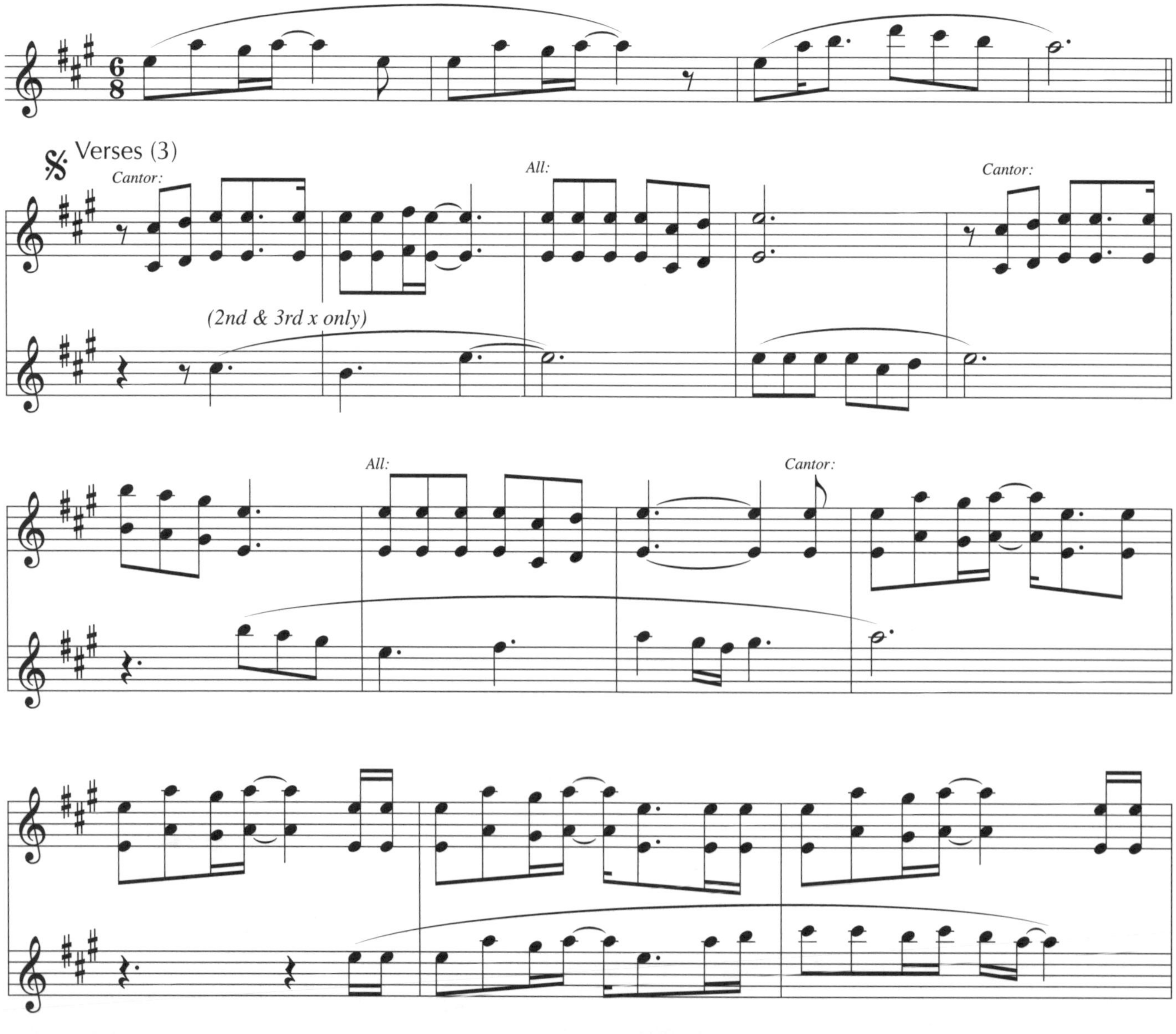

Verses (3)
Cantor:
All:
Cantor:
(2nd & 3rd x only)
All:
Cantor:

Refrain
(begin here 1st x through refrain)
(tacet last time)
7
1., 2.
D.S.
3.

746 All People That on Earth Do Dwell

Tune: OLD HUNDREDTH, LM; Louis Bourgeois, c.1510-1561
Descant: Robert J. Powell, b.1932,

An alternate descant may be found at number 407.

747 Come, Host of Heaven's High Dwelling Place

Tune: ST. COLUMBA, 8 6 8 6; Irish traditional; arr. by John L. Bell, b.1949,

Tune: BUNESSAN, 5 5 5 4 D; Gaelic, acc. by Robert J. Batastini, b.1942, (RJB)

749 This Day God Gives Me

Tune: BEACH SPRING, 8 7 8 7 D; *The Sacred Harp*, 1844; harm. by Marty Haugen, b.1950, © 1985, GIA Publications, Inc.
Instrument part: Marty Haugen, b.1950, © 1997, GIA Publications, Inc.

751 Day Is Done

Tune: AR HYD Y NOS, 8 4 8 4 888 4; Welsh (RS)

Tune: EVENING HYMN, 5 5 5 4 D; David Haas, b.1957, © 1985, GIA Publications, Inc.

753 Watch, O Lord

Refrain

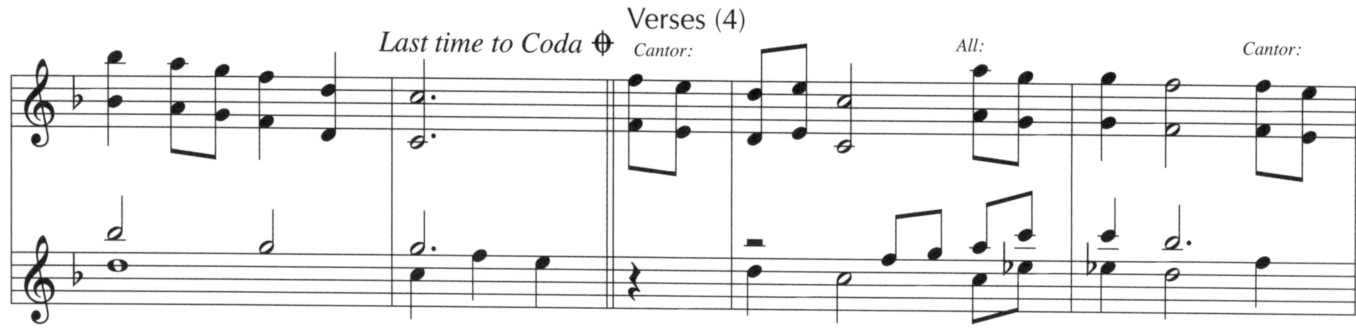

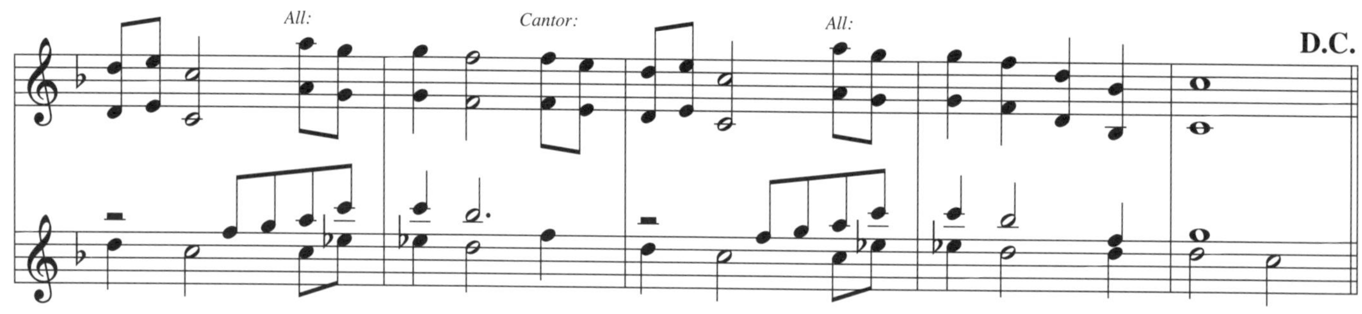

Coda *(Coda may also be used as an introduction.)*

Tune: BUNESSAN, 5 5 5 4 D; Gaelic, acc. by Robert J. Batastini, b.1942, (RJB)

755 The Trumpet in the Morning

*Cues for vss. 4–6

Tune: MORNING TRUMPET, 15 11 15 11 with refrain; B.F. White, 1800-1879, from *Southern Harmony;* arr. by Rory Cooney, b.1952,

757 O Holy City, Seen of John

(4 stanzas)

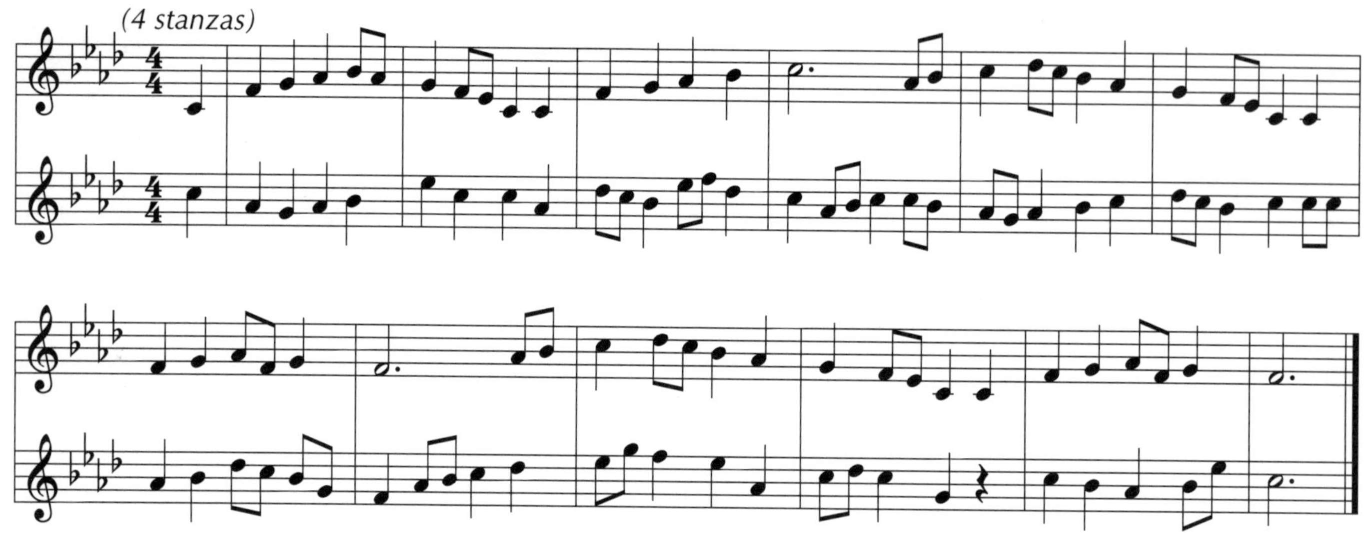

Tune: MORNING SONG, 8 6 8 6 8 6; *Kentucky Harmony,* 1816; harm. by C. Winfred Douglas, 1867-1944, © 1940, The Church Pension Fund (RS)

758 Soon and Very Soon

(4 stanzas)

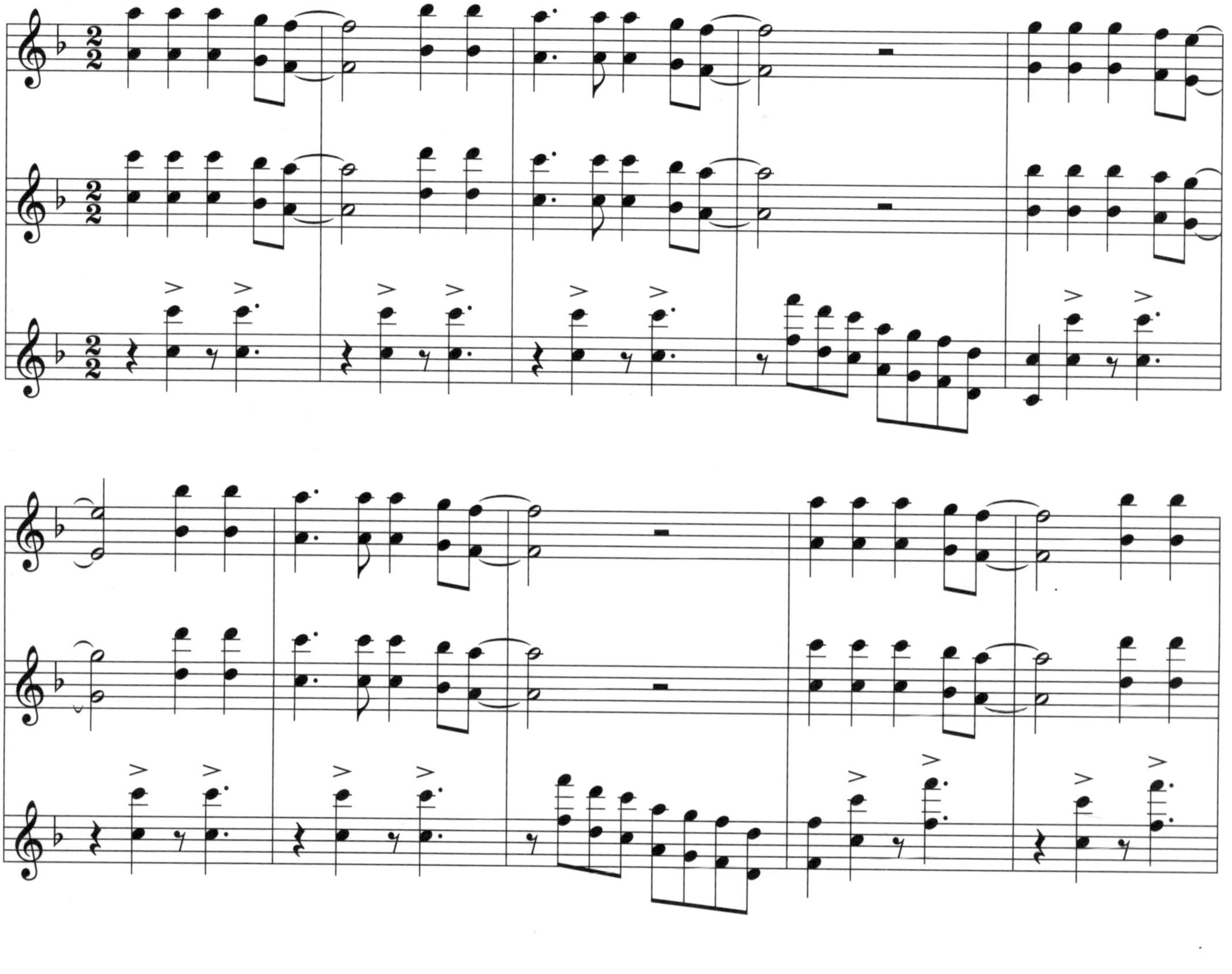

Tune: Andraé Crouch, b.1945,

759 Mine Eyes Have Seen the Glory

Tune: BATTLE HYMN OF THE REPUBLIC, 15 15 15 6 with refrain; attr. to William Steffe, d.1911
Descant: Austin C. Lovelace, b.1919, © 1992, GIA Publications, Inc.

Refrain
Last time
Last time
Verses (3)
D.C.

This page has been intentionally left blank.

761 Shall We Gather at the River

Tune: HANSON PLACE, 8 7 8 7 with refrain; Robert Lowry, 1826-1899

762 We Shall Rise Again

Tune RESURRECTION; Irregular with refrain; Jeremy Young, b.1948, © 1987, GIA Publications, Inc.

763 I Will Be the Vine

D.C.

Verse 3

D.C.

Tune: Liam Lawton, b.1959; arr. by John McCann, b.1961, © 1998, GIA Publications, Inc.

Jerusalem, My Happy Home 764

(6 stanzas)

Tune: LAND OF REST, CM; American; harm. by Richard Proulx, b.1937, © 1975, GIA Publications, Inc.
Descant: Richard Proulx, b.1937, © 1997, GIA Publications, Inc.

765 Do Not Let Your Hearts Be Troubled

Verses 2, 3
D.C.

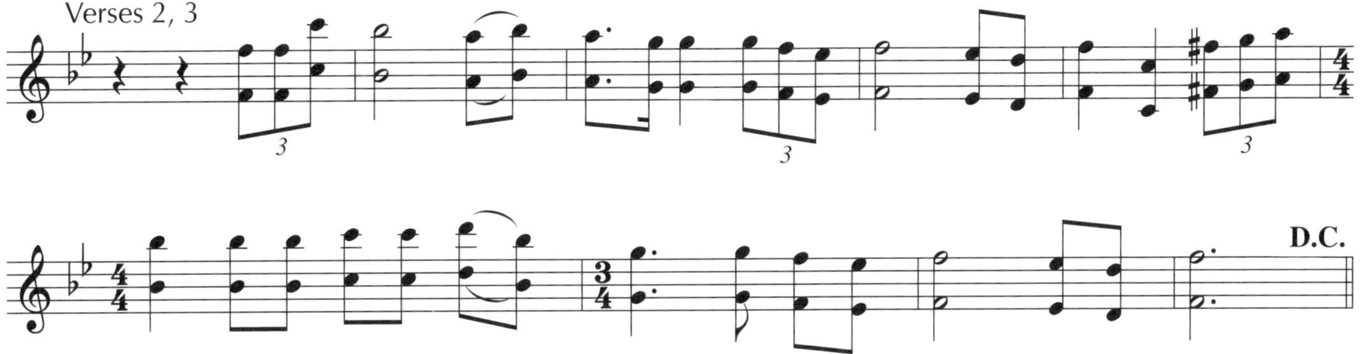

Tune: David Haas, b.1957, © 1995, GIA Publications, Inc.

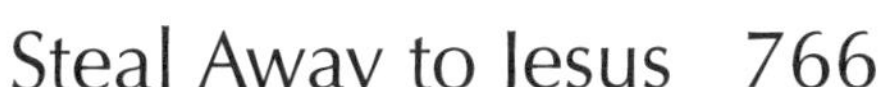

Steal Away to Jesus 766

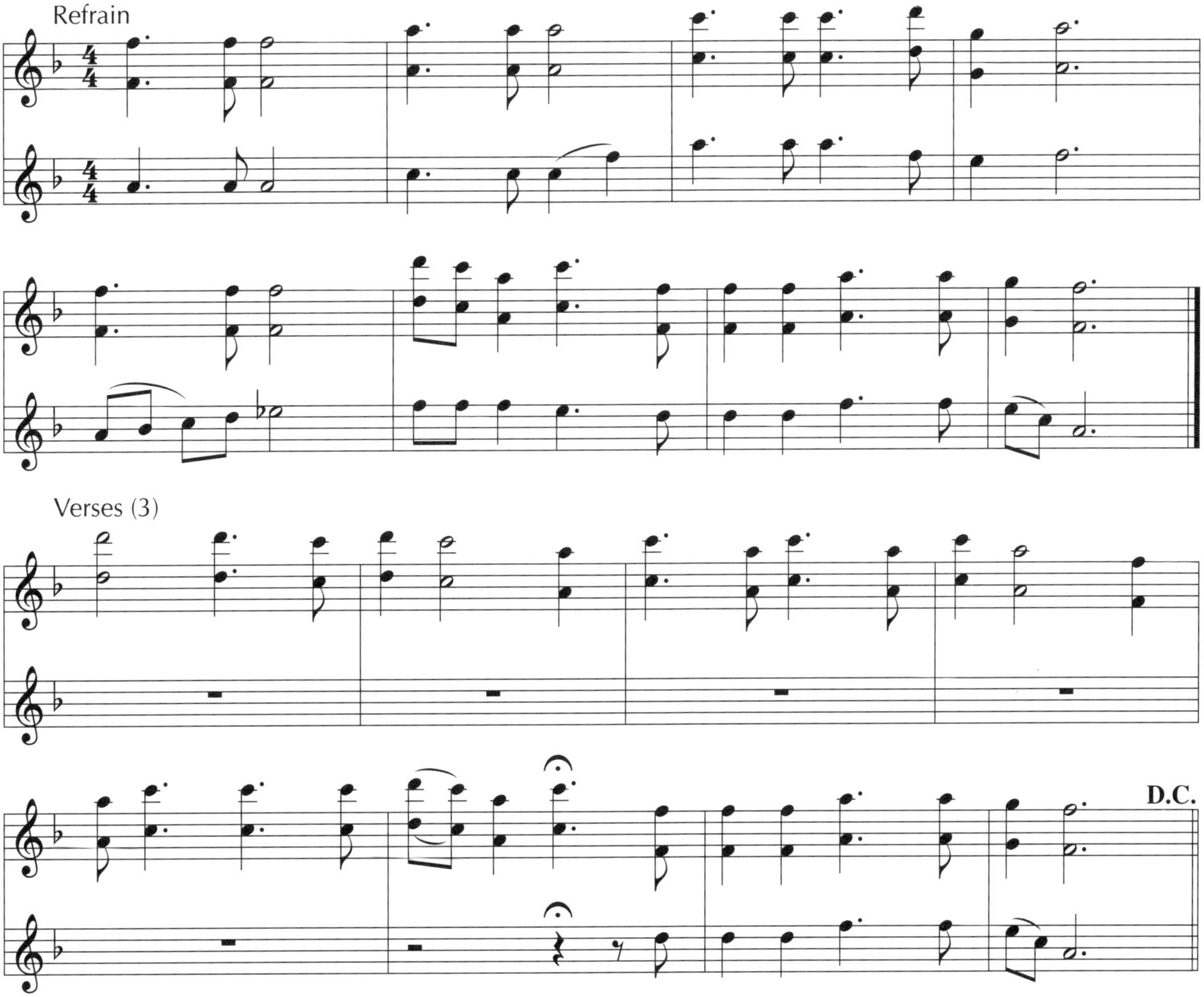
Refrain
Verses (3)
D.C.

Tune: African-American spiritual

768 No Wind at the Window

(4 stanzas)

Tune: COLUMCILLE, Irregular; Gaelic, arr. by John L. Bell, b.1949, © 1992, Iona Community, GIA Publications, Inc., agent (JM)

769 Praise We the Lord This Day

(6 stanzas)

Tune: SWABIA, SM; Johann M. Speiss, 1715-1772; adapt. by William H. Havergal, 1793-1870
Descant: Richard Proulx, b.1937, © 1979, GIA Publications, Inc.

Transform Us 770

(3 stanzas)

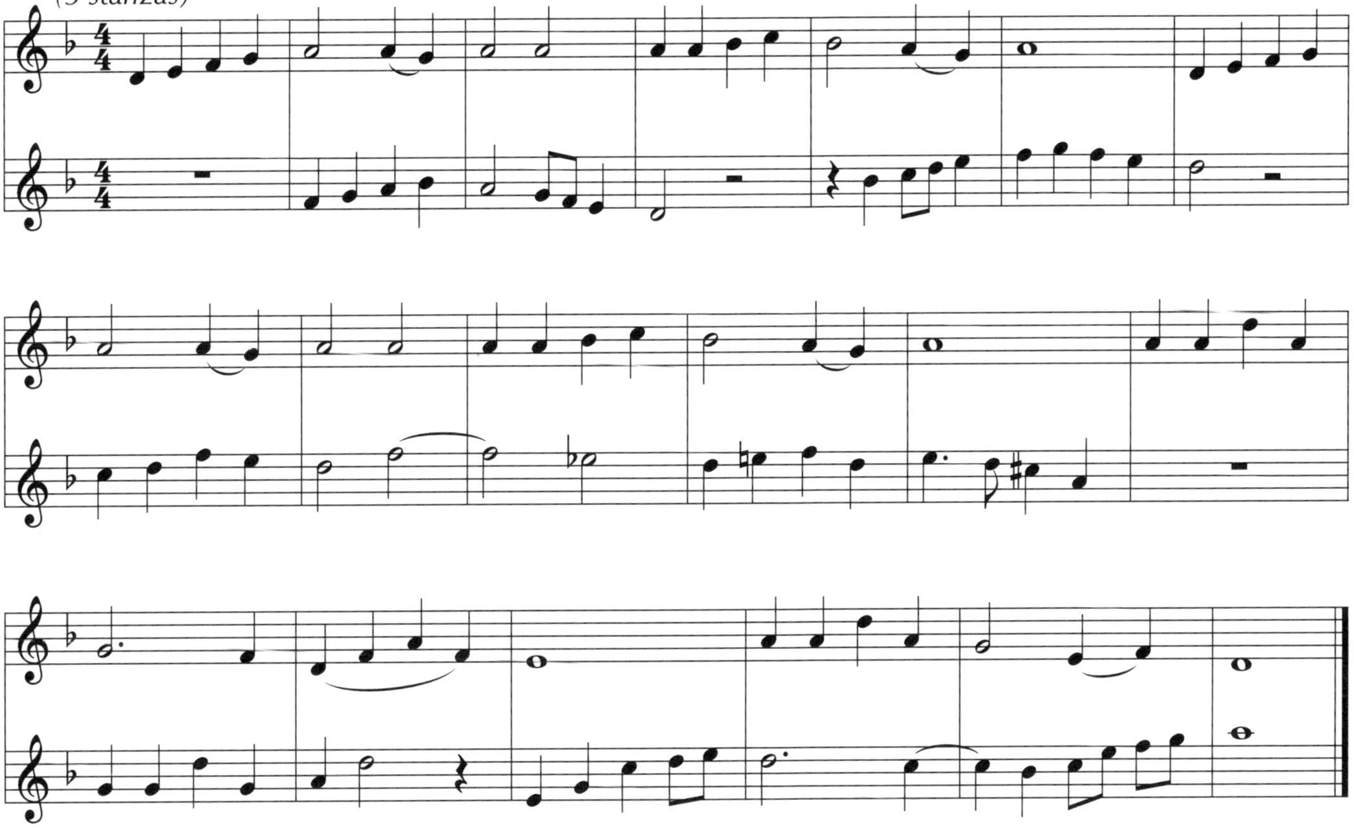

Tune: PICARDY, 8 7 8 7 8 7; French Carol; harm. by Richard Proulx, b.1937, © 1986, GIA Publications, Inc. (JM)

'Tis Good, Lord, to Be Here 771

(5 stanzas)

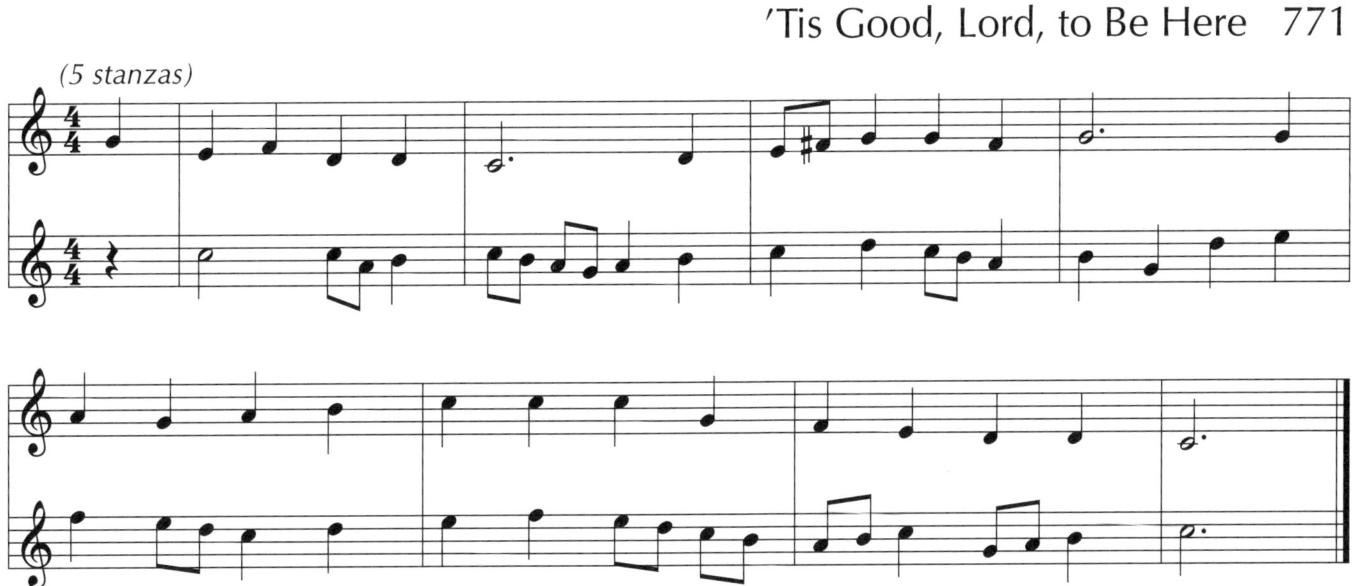

Tune: SWABIA, SM; Johann M. Speiss, 1715-1772; adapt. by William H. Havergal, 1793-1870
Descant: Richard Proulx, b.1937, © 1979, GIA Publications, Inc.

772 Ave Maria

Tune: Dan Kantor, b.1960; arr. by Rob Glover, b.1950, © 1993, GIA Publications, Inc.

773 Magnificat

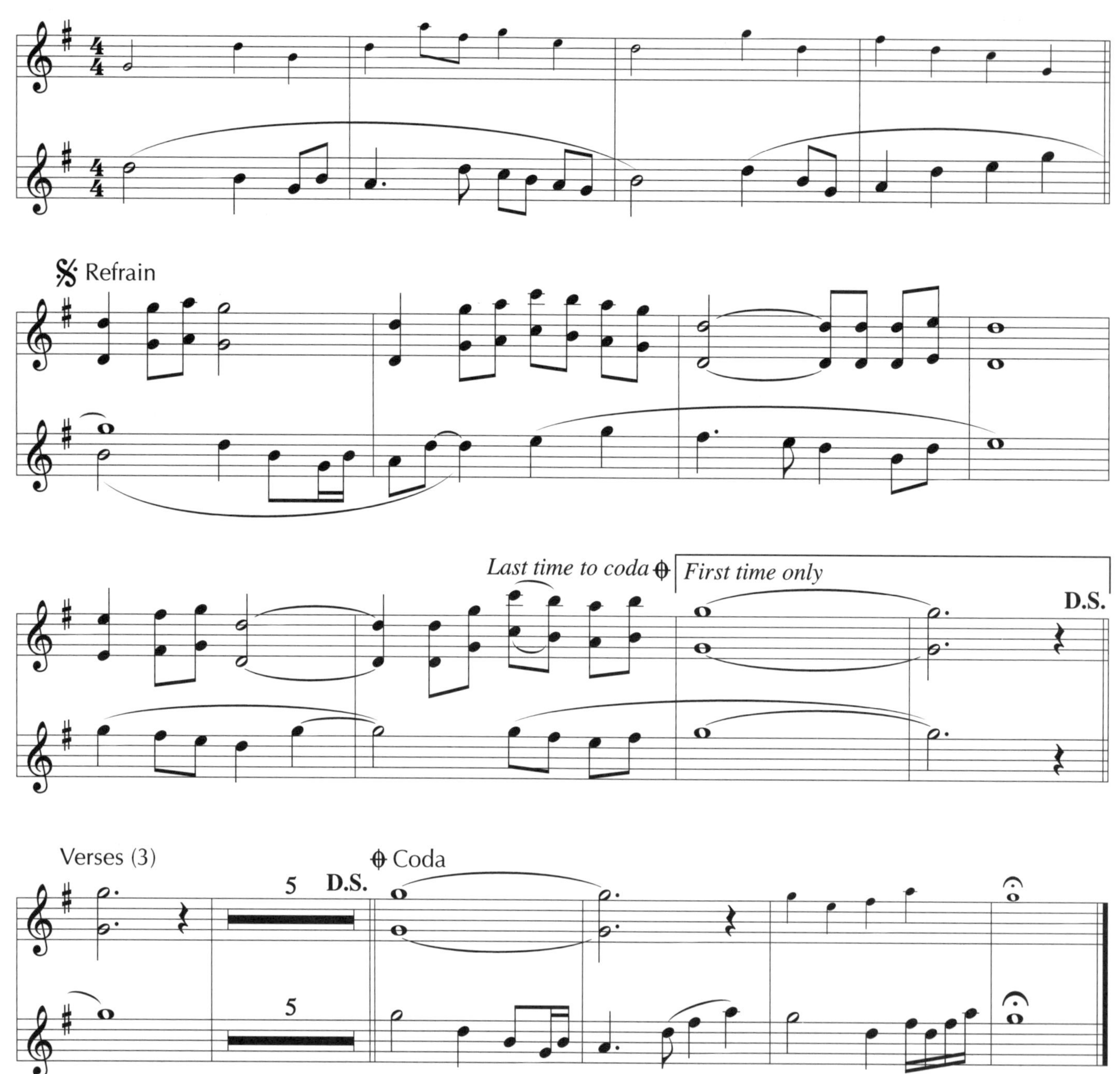

Tune: David Haas, b.1957, © 1990, GIA Publications, Inc.

O Sanctissima / O Most Virtuous 775

Tune: O DU FRÖLICHE, 55 7 55 7; Tattersall's *Improved Psalmody*, 1794 (RS)

Sing We of the Blessed Mother 776

Tune: OMNE DIE, 8 7 8 7 D; *Trier Gesängbuch*, 1695

777 I Sing a Maid

Tune: THE FLIGHT OF THE EARLS; CMD; traditional Celtic melody; harm. by Michael Joncas, b.1951, © 1987, GIA Publications, Inc.
Instrument part: Michael Joncas, b.1951, © 1997, GIA Publications, Inc.

*Four verses for the Feast of the Holy Family.

Tune: PLEADING SAVIOR, 8 7 8 7 D; *Christian Lyre,* 1830; harm. by Richard Proulx, b.1937, © 1986, GIA Publications, Inc.
Descant: Richard Proulx, b.1937, © 1997, GIA Publications, Inc.

779 Hail Mary: Gentle Woman

Tune: Carey Landry, b.1944
Instrument part: Kevin Keil, b.1956

This page has been intentionally left blank.

Tune: SIOBHAN NI LAOGHAIRE, 11 12 11 11; Gaelic folk hymn; arr. by Steven C. Warner, b.1954,

782 My Soul Proclaims

Tune: Marty Haugen, b.1950, © 2001, GIA Publications, Inc.

Immaculate Mary 783

(7 stanzas)

Tune: LOURDES HYMN, 11 11 with refrain; *Grenoble,* 1882
Descant: Frank Chierico, © 1980, GIA Publications, Inc.

784 Hail, Holy Queen Enthroned Above

Tune: SALVE REGINA COELITUM, 8 4 8 4 777 4 5; *Choralmelodien zum Heiligen Gesänge,* 1808; harm. by Healey Willan, 1880-1968, (RS)

Tune: CRUCIFER, 10 10 with refrain; Sydney H. Nicholson, 1875-1947, © 1974, Hope Publishing Co. (RS)

786 For All the Saints Who've Shown Your Love

Tune: O WALY WALY, LM; English; harm. by John L. Bell, b.1949,

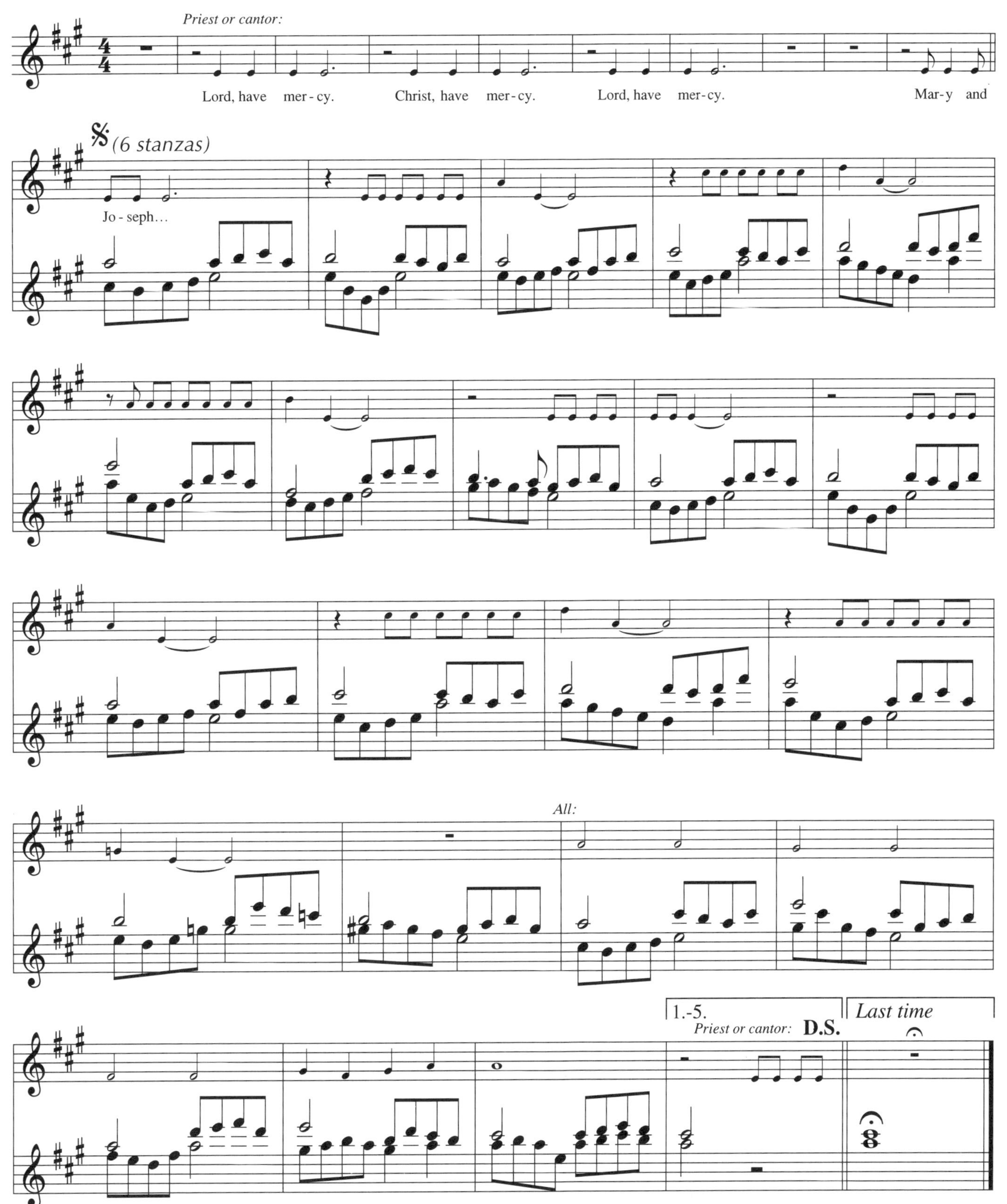

Tune: John D. Becker, b.1953, © 1987. Published by OCP Publications.

789 For the Faithful Who Have Answered

Tune: WE GIVE YOU THANKS, 8 7 8 7 D with refrain; David Haas, b.1957, © 1998, GIA Publications, Inc.

790 Ye Watchers and Ye Holy Ones

Tune: LASST UNS ERFREUEN, LM; with alleluias; *Geistliche Kirchengasange,* Cologne, 1623; harm. by Ralph Vaughan Williams, 1872-1958,

Tune: SINE NOMINE, 10 10 10 with alleluias; Ralph Vaughan Williams, 1872-1958, © Oxford University Press
Descant: Harold Owen, b.1931, © 1979, GIA Publications, Inc.

792 For the Life of the World

Tune: David Haas, b.1957; acc. by Jeanne Cotter, b.1964, © 1993, GIA Publications, Inc.

Who Calls You by Name 794

Refrain

Cantor: *All:* *Cantor:* *All:*

Cantor: *All:* *Last time*

Last time

Verses (3)

*

D.C.

**Cues for vs. 3*

Tune: David Haas, b.1957, © 1988, GIA Publications, Inc.

795 Christ Will Be Your Strength

Tune: David Haas, b.1957, © 1988, GIA Publications, Inc.

796 There Is One Lord

Simple Melody

Flute

Oboe

Tune: Jacques Berthier, 1923-1994, © 1984, Les Presses de Taizé, GIA Publications, Inc., agent

Tune: BUNESSAN, 5 5 8 D; Gaelic; acc. by Marty Haugen, b.1950, © 1987, GIA Publications, Inc.
Descant: Marty Haugen, b.1950, © 1997, GIA Publications, Inc.

798 Covenant Hymn

(5 stanzas)

*Choose either part

Tune: LAND OF REST, CM; American; harm. by Annabel M. Buchanan, 1888-1983, © 1938, 1966, J. Fisher and Bro. (RS)

O Breathe on Me, O Breath of God 800

Tune: ST. COLUMBA, CM; Gaelic; harm. by A. Gregory Murray, OSB, 1905-1992, © Downside Abbey
Descant: John Ferguson, b.1941, © 1992, GIA Publications, Inc.

This page has been intentionally left blank.

Tune: APPALACHIAN FALL, 11 11 11 11; William P. Rowan, b.1951, © 2002, GIA Publications, Inc.

Refrain
Cantor:
All:
Cantor:
All:
Cantor:
All:
Cantor:
All:
To verses
(lead in to line 3 of verses)

Tune: Bob Moore, b.1962, © 1999, GIA Publications, Inc.

803 Bread of Life from Heaven / Pan de Vida Eterna

Tune: Argentine folk melody; adapt. and verses by Marty Haugen, b.1950, © 2001, GIA Publications, Inc.

Refrain
Verses (10)
D.C.

806 Eat This Bread

Tune: Jacques Berthier, 1923-1994, © 1984, Les Presses de Taizé, GIA Publications, Inc., agent

Refrain
Verses (10) 5 in English, 5 in Spanish
D.C.

808 Let Us Be Bread

Verse 1
D.C.
Verse 2
D.C.
Verse 3
D.C.
Verse 4
D.C.

This page has been intentionally left blank.

Tune: LIVING GOD, 7 7 7 7 with refrain; Anonymous; harm. by Richard Proulx, b.1937, © 1986, GIA Publications, Inc.
Instrument part: Richard Proulx, b.1937, © 1997, GIA Publications, Inc.

810 Come to the Banquet

Refrain

tr

To verses

Last time

tr

tr

Verses (4)

Tune: James J. Chepponis, b.1956, © 2000, GIA Publications, Inc.

811 Pan de Vida

1.- 3.
To verses
Last time
Verses (3)
D.C.

812 Take and Eat

D.C.

813 One Bread, One Body

Verses (3)

Coda
D.C.

814 We Come to Your Feast

815 Joyous Cup: A Processional for the Easter Season

Verses (9) *(Three lines are not meant to be played together.)*

Refrain
Verses (5)
D.C.

817 All Who Hunger

Tune: Bob Moore, b. 1962, © 1993, GIA Publications, Inc.

818 Shepherd of Souls

Tune: ST. AGNES, CM; John B. Dykes, 1823-1876; harm. by Richard Proulx, b.1937, © 1986, GIA Publications, Inc.

819 In Remembrance of You

Verses (3)

Tune: Paul A. Tate, b.1968, © 1997, World Library Publications

820 Come and Eat This Living Bread

Tune: James J. Chepponis, b.1956, © 1987, GIA Publications, Inc.

822 I Am the Bread of Life / Yo Soy el Pan de Vida

Refrain
Last time
Last time
Last time
Verses (7)
Cantor:
All:
D.S.

824 Behold the Lamb

Tune: Martin Willett, b.1960; acc. by Craig S. Kingsbury, b.1952
Instrument part: Randall De Bruyn

825 Now in This Banquet

*May be played in canon.

Verse 3
D.C.
Verse 4
D.C.
Verse 5
D.C.
Verse 6
D.C.

826 Alleluia! Sing to Jesus

Tune: HYFRYDOL, 8 7 8 7 D; Rowland H. Prichard, 1811-1887

Tune: James E. Moore, Jr., b.1951, © 1983, GIA Publications, Inc.

828 The Hand of God

Verse 3
D.C.

829 Draw Near

Tune: Dan Feiten, b.1953; keyboard arr. by Eric Gunnison, and R.J. Miller, © 1987, Ekklesia Music, Inc.

831 Come and Eat This Bread

*Play only when leading into final 2 bars.

Verses (5)
D.C.

Tune: Marty Haugen, b.1950,

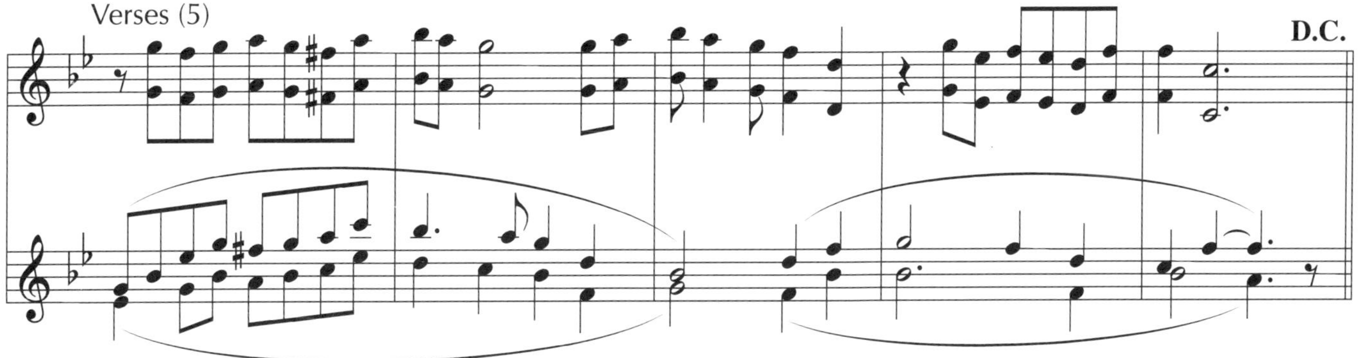

Let Us Break Bread Together 832

Verses (3)
Refrain

Tune: LET US BREAK BREAD, 10 10 6 8 7; American folk hymn; harm. by David Hurd, b.1950,

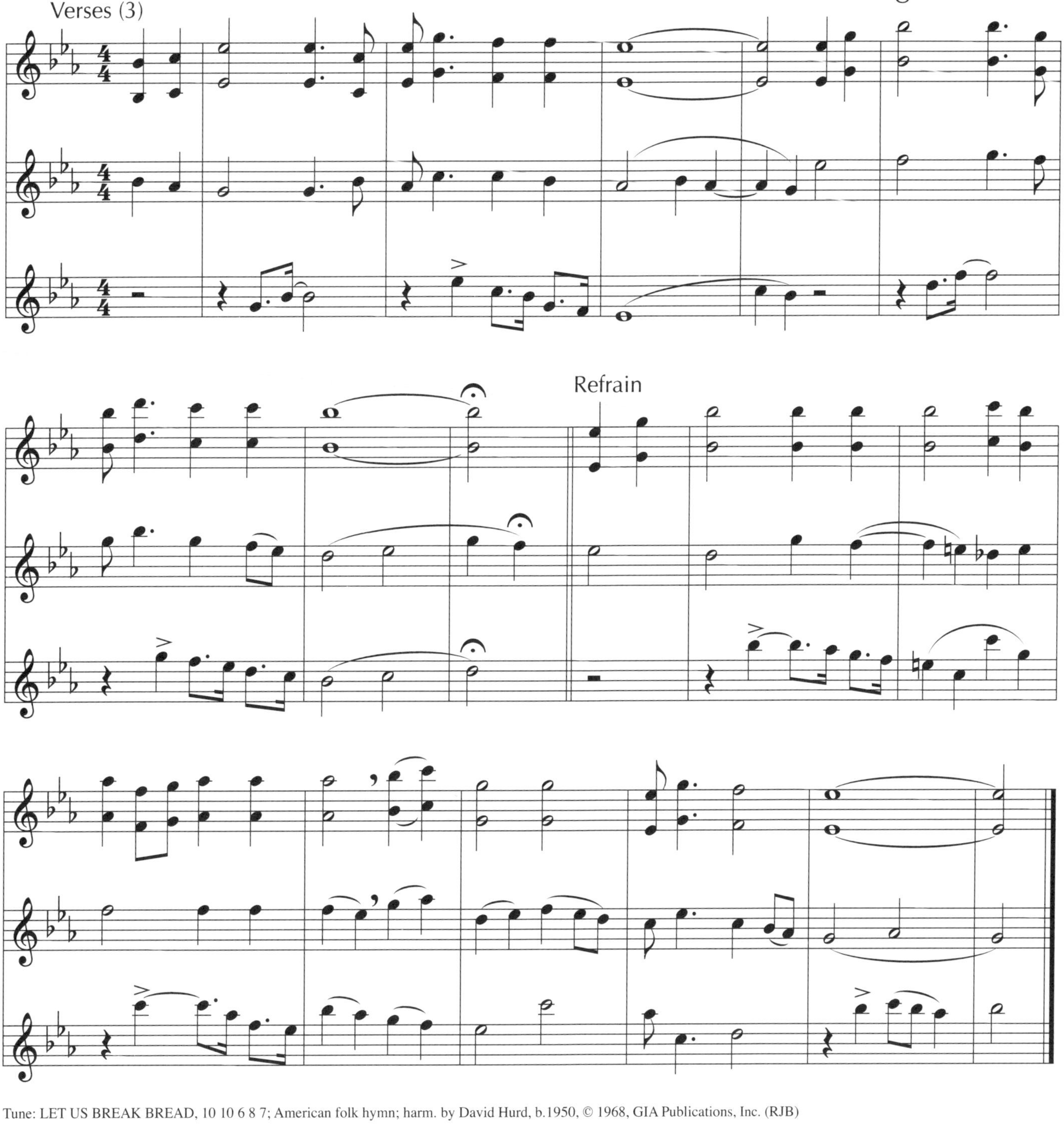

833 Table Song

Tune: David Haas, b. 1957, © 1991, GIA Publications, Inc.

Tune: Rory Cooney, b.1952, © 1987, North American Liturgy Resources. Published by OCP Publications.

836 We Remember, We Believe

Tune: Thomas J. Porter, b.1958, © 1997, GIA Publications, Inc.

837 Look Beyond

Tune: Darryl Ducote, b.1945, © 1969, 1979, Damean Music. Distributed by GIA Publications, Inc.

Tune: David Haas, b.1957, © 2003, GIA Publications, Inc.

839 Take and Eat This Bread

Tune: Francis Patrick O'Brien, b.1958, © 1992, GIA Publications, Inc.

Tune: UNDE ET MEMORES, 10 10 10 10 with refrain; William H. Monk, 1823-1889, alt. (RS)

841 The Living Bread of God

D.C.

Tune: Kate Cuddy, b.1953, © 1992, GIA Publications, Inc. (JM)

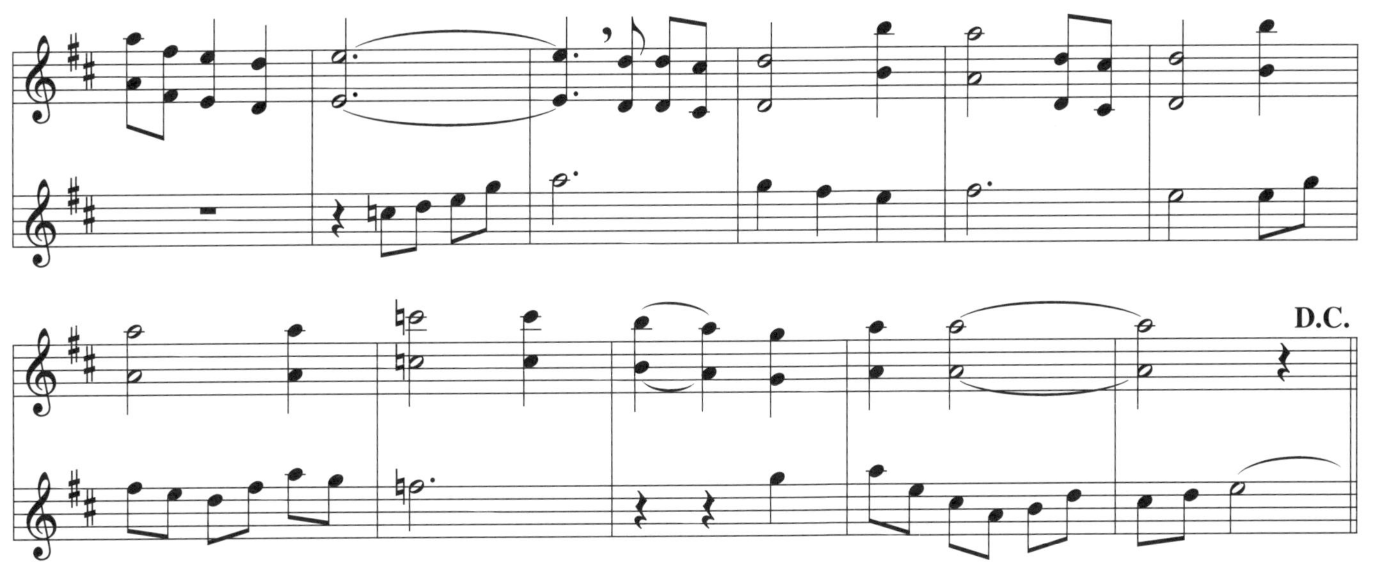

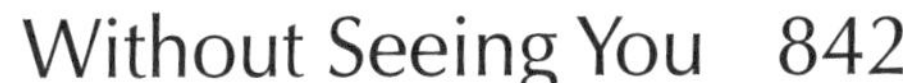

Without Seeing You 842

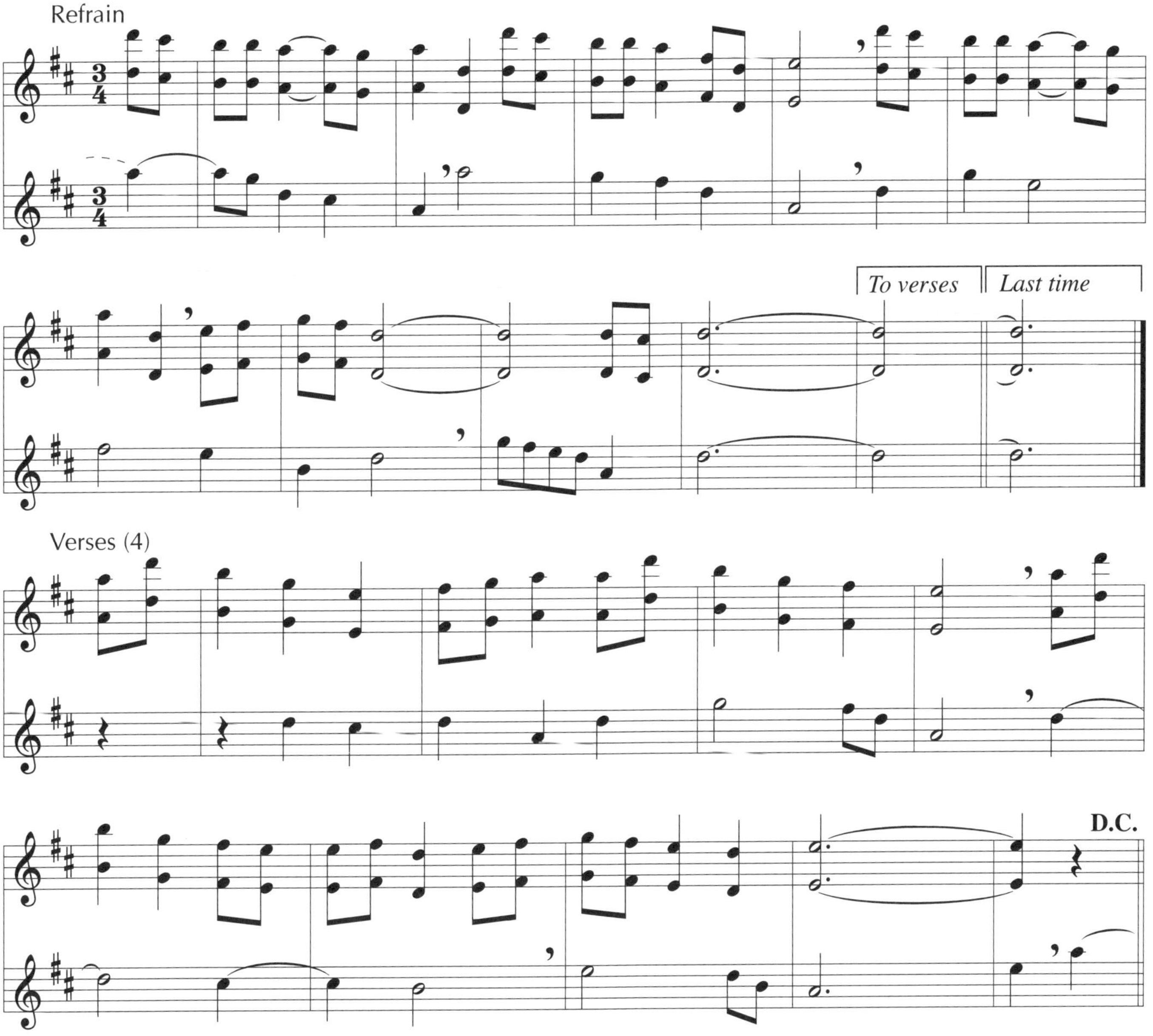
Refrain
To verses
Last time
Verses (4)
D.C.

Tune: David Haas, b.1957, © 1993, GIA Publications, Inc.

843 In the Breaking of the Bread / Cuando Partimos el Pan del Señor

Tune: Bob Hurd, b.1950, © 1984, Bob Hurd; acc. by Dominic MacAller, b.1959
Instrument part: Craig S. Kingsbury, b.1952, © 1984, OCP Publications
Published by OCP Publications

He Healed the Darkness of My Mind 844

(3 stanzas)

1., 2.

3.

Tune: ARLINGTON, LM; David Haas, b.1957, © 1988, GIA Publications, Inc.

845 Hands of Healing

Canon

1.

2.

3.

Repeat as needed

Tune: Marty Haugen, b.1950, © 1999, GIA Publications, Inc.

846 Jesus, Heal Us

Verse 2
D.C.
Verse 3
D.C.

Verse 4

Tune: PRECIOUS LORD, 66 9 D; George N. Allen, 1812-1877; arr. by Kelly Dobbs Mickus, b.1966, © 1938, Unichappell Music, Inc. (JM)

848 Forgive Our Sins

Tune: DETROIT, CM; Supplement to *Kentucky Harmony,* 1820; harm. by Gerald H. Knight, 1908-1979, © The Royal School of Church Music
Descant: Richard Hillert, b.1923, © 1992, GIA Publications, Inc.

849 Our Father, We Have Wandered

Tune: PASSION CHORALE, 7 6 7 6 D; Hans Leo Hassler, 1564-1612; harm. by J. S. Bach, 1685-1750 (RS)

Tune: Will L. Thompson, 1847-1909 (RS)

851 Remember Your Love

Tune: Tom Conry, b.1951, © 1978, OCP Publications

853 The Master Came to Bring Good News

Tune: ICH GLAUB AN GOTT, 8 7 8 7 with refrain; *Mainz Gesangbuch,* 1870; harm. by Richard Proulx, b.1937, © 1986, GIA Publications, Inc.
Descant: Richard Proulx, b.1937, © 1997, GIA Publications, Inc.

Tune: Marty Haugen, b.1950, © 1987, GIA Publications, Inc.

855 Love Is the Sunlight

Tune: SHADE, 5 5 5 4 D; David Haas, b.1957,

Tune: O WALY WALY, LM; English; harm. by Martin West, b.1929, © 1983, Hope Publishing Co.
Descant: Robert A. Hobby, © 1992, GIA Publications, Inc.

857 Wherever You Go

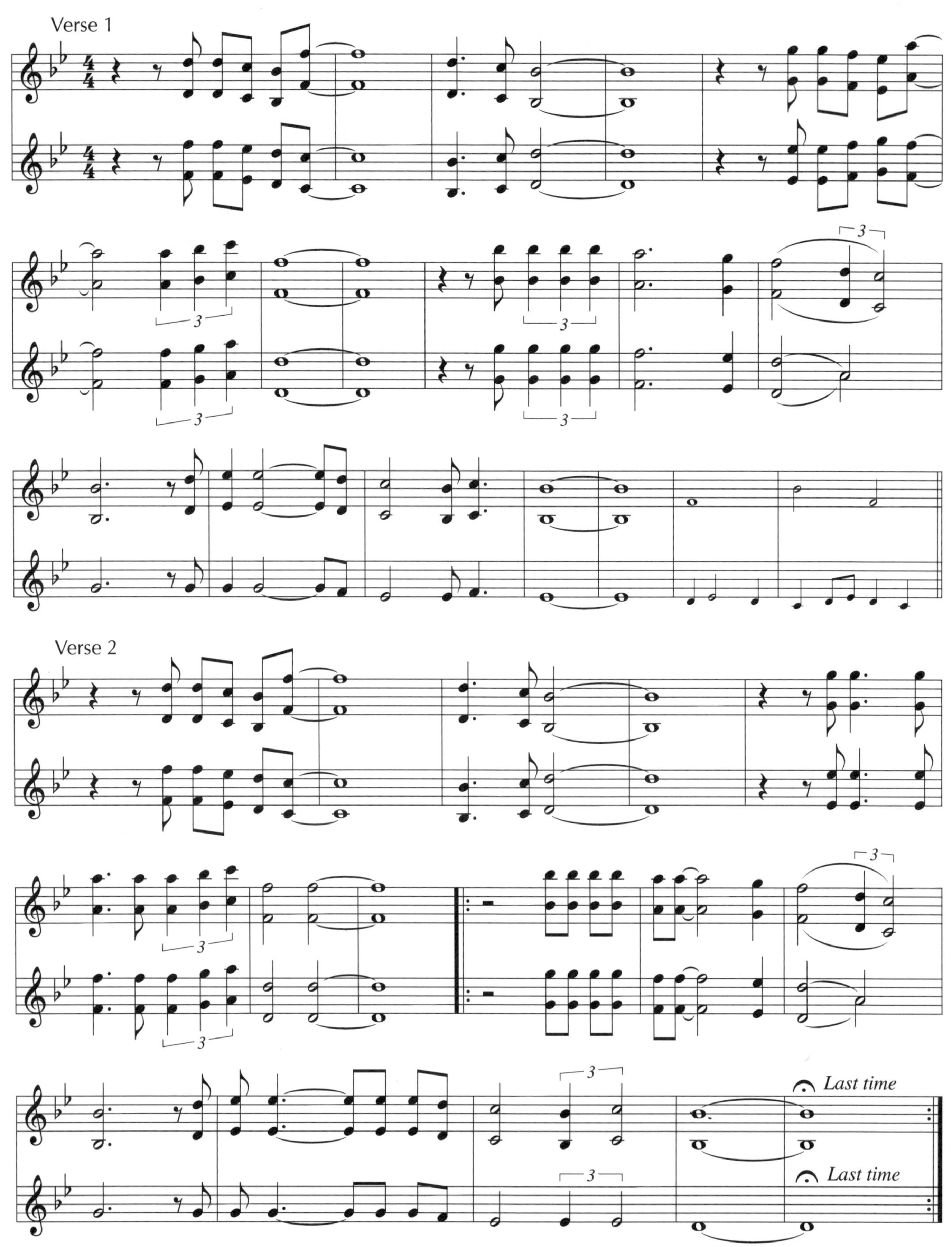

Tune: SLANE, 10 10 10 10; Irish traditional; harm. by Erik Routley, 1917-1982, © 1975, Hope Publishing Co.
Descant: Richard Proulx, b.1937, © 1979, GIA Publications, Inc.

This page has been intentionally left blank.

Tune: Michael Joncas, b.1951, © 1989, GIA Publications, Inc.

860 Wherever You Go

Verse 3
D.S.

862 The Hand of God Shall Hold You

Tune: Marty Haugen, b.1950, © 1994, GIA Publications, Inc.

863 I Know That My Redeemer Lives

Tune: David Haas, b.1957, © 1990, GIA Publications, Inc.

The Last Journey 864

(4 stanzas)

Tune: IONA BOAT SONG, 12 9 12 9; Scottish traditional; arr. by John L. Bell, b.1949, © 1989, 1996, Iona Community, GIA Publications, Inc., agent

867 Song of Farewell

Verse 3
D.C.
Verse 4
D.C.
Alternate children's verse 4
D.C.

This page has been intentionally left blank.

Tune: LONDONDERRY AIR, 11 10 11 10 D; arr. by John L. Bell, b.1949,

869 There Is a Place

2.-4.
Refrain
To verses
D.S.
Final ending

870 God of Adam, God of Joseph /
871 God of Eve and God of Mary

Tune: FARRELL, 8 7 8 7 with refrain; Thomas J. Porter, b.1958,

Tune: MATERNA, CMD; Samuel A. Ward, 1848-1903
Descant: Irving Lauf, © 1980, GIA Publications, Inc.

873 Star-Spangled Banner

Tune: STAR SPANGLED BANNER, Irregular; John S. Smith, 1750-1836

Tune: AMERICA, 66 4 666 4; *Thesaurus Musicus,* 1744
Descant: Austin C. Lovelace, b.1919,

875 This Is My Song

(3 stanzas)

Tune: FINLANDIA, 11 10 11 10 11 10; Jean Sibelius, 1865-1957 (RS)

876 We Have a Dream

(6 stanzas)

Tune: NATIONAL HYMN, 10 10 10 10; George W. Warren, 1828-1902
Descant: Sam Batt Owens, 1928-1998, © 1980, GIA Publications, Inc.

The God of All Eternity 877

(5 stanzas)

Tune: O WALY WALY, LM; English; harm. by John L. Bell, b.1949, © 1989, Iona Community, GIA Publications, Inc., agent (RJB)

SERVICE MUSIC

All music found from nos. 86 to 322 is copyright by GIA Publications, Inc., with the exception of those items specified below. Please refer to nos. 86 to 322 for specific copyright dates.

2 © 1987, GIA Publications, Inc.
5 Harm.: © 1987, GIA Publications, Inc.
13 © 1979, 1988, GIA Publications, Inc.
18 © 1993, GIA Publications, Inc.
19 Music: © 1988, 1994, GIA Publications, Inc. Instrument part: © 2005, GIA Publications, Inc.
20 Music: © 1983, GIA Publications, Inc. Descant: © 1996, GIA Publications, Inc.
21 © 2003, GIA Publications, Inc.
23 © 1986, GIA Publications, Inc.
25 © 1993, GIA Publications, Inc.
26 © 1982, GIA Publications, Inc.
27 © 1985, GIA Publications, Inc.
28 © 2000, GIA Publications, Inc.
29 Music: © 1983, GIA Publications, Inc. Instrument part: © 2005, GIA Publications, Inc.
30 © 1985, Paul Inwood. Published by OCP Publications. P.O. Box 13248, Portland, OR 97213-0248. All rights reserved. Used with permission.
31 © 1993, GIA Publications, Inc.
32 © 1987, GIA Publications, Inc.
33 Music: © 1978, 1990, John B. Foley, SJ, and OCP Publications. Instrument part: © 2005, OCP Publications. P.O. Box 13248, Portland, OR 97213-0248. All rights reserved. Used with permission.
34 © 1996, GIA Publications, Inc.
35 © 1971, 1991, North American Liturgy Resources. Published by OCP Publications. P.O. Box 13248, Portland, OR 97213-0248. All rights reserved. Used with permission.
37 Music: © 1987, GIA Publications, Inc. Instrument part: © 2005, GIA Publications, Inc.
38 © 2003, GIA Publications, Inc.
39 © 1998, GIA Publications, Inc.
41 Music: © 1983, GIA Publications, Inc. Instrument part: © 2005, GIA Publications, Inc.
42 © 1982, GIA Publications, Inc.
43 © 1987, GIA Publications, Inc.
45 © 1984, GIA Publications, Inc.
46 © 1987, 1994, GIA Publications, Inc.
47 © 1982, GIA Publications, Inc.
49 Music: © 1988, 1994, GIA Publications, Inc. Instrument part: © 2005, GIA Publications, Inc.
50 © 1980, GIA Publications, Inc.
51 © 1983, 1994, GIA Publications, Inc.
52 © 1976, GIA Publications, Inc.
53 © 1998, GIA Publications, Inc.
54 © 1989, 1994, GIA Publications, Inc.
55 © 1983, 1994, GIA Publications, Inc.
56 © 1983, GIA Publications, Inc.
58 © 1993, GIA Publications, Inc.
61 © 2003, GIA Publications, Inc.
62 © 1987, GIA Publications, Inc.
66 © 1979, GIA Publications, Inc.
67 © 2001, GIA Publications, Inc.
68 © 1987, GIA Publications, Inc
69 © 1988, GIA Publications, Inc.
70 Music: © 1987, 1993, GIA Publications, Inc. Instrument part: © 2005, GIA Publications, Inc.
71 Music: © 1983, GIA Publications, Inc. Instrument part: © 2005, GIA Publications, Inc.
72 Music: © 1985, GIA Publications, Inc. Instrument part: © 2005, GIA Publications, Inc.
75 © 1990, GIA Publications, Inc.
76 Music: © 1983, GIA Publications, Inc. Instrument part: © 2005, GIA Publications, Inc.
77 Music: © 1987, GIA Publications, Inc. Instrument part: © 2005, GIA Publications, Inc.
79 © 1997, GIA Publications, Inc.
80 © 1992, GIA Publications, Inc.
81 © 1988, 1994, GIA Publications, Inc.
82 © 2002, World Library Publications, a division of J.S. Paluch Company, Inc. Schiller Park, IL 60176. All rights reserved. Used by permission.
83 Music: © 1989, GIA Publications, Inc. Instrument part: © 2005, GIA Publications, Inc.
84 © 1980, GIA Publications, Inc.
85 © 2003, GIA Publications, Inc.
253 © 1979, 1988, Les Presses de Taizé, GIA Publications, Inc., agent
266 © 1985, Fintan O'Carroll and Christopher Walker. Published by OCP Publications. P.O. Box 13248, Portland, OR 97213-0248. All rights reserved. Used with permission.
293 Music adapt.: ©1980, Church Pension Fund. Used by permission of Church Publishing Incorporated, New York. Instrument part: © 2005, GIA Publications, Inc.
313 © 1973, Robert J. Dufford, SJ and Daniel L. Schutte. Published by OCP Publications. P.O. Box 13248, Portland, OR 97213-0248. All rights reserved. Used with permission.
315 © 1973, Robert J. Dufford, SJ and Daniel L. Schutte. Published by OCP Publications. P.O. Box 13248, Portland, OR 97213-0248. All rights reserved. Used with permission.
324 © 1999, GIA Publications, Inc.
325 © 1990, GIA Publications, Inc.
326 © 2001, GIA Publications, Inc.
328 © 1990, Paul Inwood. Published and distributed by World Library Publications, a division of J.S. Paluch Company, Inc. Schiller Park, IL 60176. All rights reserved. Used by permission.
329 © 1988, GIA Publications, Inc.
330 © 1984, Les Presses de Taizé, GIA Publications, Inc., agent
331 Descant: © 1992, GIA Publications, Inc.
332 © 1976, Robert J. Dufford, SJ, and OCP Publications, P.O. Box 13248, Portland, OR 97213-0248. All rights reserved. Used with permission.
333 Harm: © 1958, Basilian Fathers, assigned to Ralph Jusko Publications, Inc.
335 © 1996, GIA Publications, Inc.
336 © 1982, GIA Publications, Inc.
337 Harm.: from *The Oxford Book of Carols,* © Oxford University Press. Descant: © 1992, GIA Publications, Inc.
338 © 1995, GIA Publications, Inc.
339 © 2000, GIA Publications, Inc.
340 © 1984, Les Presses de Taizé, GIA Publications, Inc., agent
341 © 2001, Iona Community, GIA Publications, Inc., agent
343 © 1981, 1982, Jan Michael Joncas Trust. Published by OCP Publications. P.O. Box 13248, Portland, OR 97213-0248. All rights reserved. Used with permission.
345 Descant: © 1979, GIA Publications, Inc.
346 © 1983, GIA Publications, Inc.
347 Arr.: © 1994, GIA Publications, Inc.
349 © 1988, GIA Publications, Inc.
350 © 1971, The United Church Press. Reprinted from *A New Song 3*. Instrument part: © 1987, GIA Publications, Inc.
351 © 1983, GIA Publications, Inc.
352 © 2000, GIA Publications, Inc.
354 © 1987, GIA Publications, Inc.
355 © 2003, GIA Publications, Inc.
358 © 2002, GIA Publications, Inc.
360 © 1992, GIA Publications, Inc.
361 Descant: © 1979, GIA Publications, Inc.
362 © 1996, GIA Publications, Inc.
363 Harm: © 1995, GIA Publications, Inc.
364 Tune tr. and arr.: © 1990, Iona Community, GIA Publications, Inc., agent
365 Harm.: © 1994, GIA Publications, Inc.
367 Descant: © 1980, GIA Publications, Inc.
368 © 1991, GIA Publications, Inc.
370 © 1985, GIA Publications, Inc.
371 Descant: © 1980, GIA Publications, Inc.
372 © 1984, GIA Publications, Inc.
376 © 2003, GIA Publications, Inc.
377 Harm.: © Bristol Churches Housing Assoc. Ltd.
378 © 1945, Boosey and Co., Ltd.; Copyright Renewed. Reprinted by permission of Boosey & Hawkes, Inc.
379 Descant: © 1982, GIA Publications, Inc.
380 Harm.: © 1957, Novello and Co. Ltd
381 © 1987, Iona Community, GIA Publications Inc., agent
384 Descant: © 1979, GIA Publications, Inc.
385 © 1978, Damean Music. Distributed by GIA Publications, Inc.
386 Harm.: © 1978, *Lutheran Book of Worship*. Administered by Augsburg Fortress. Used by permission. Instrument part: © 2002, GIA Publications, Inc.
388 Harm.: © 1961, Oxford University Press
389 Descant: © 1980, GIA Publications, Inc.
391 © 2003, GIA Publications, Inc.
392 © 1991, GIA Publications, Inc.
393 © 1991, Les Presses de Taizé, GIA Publications, Inc., agent
394 Harm.: © 1986, GIA Publications, Inc. Instrument part: © 1997, GIA Publications, Inc.
396 © 1996, GIA Publications, Inc.
397 Descant: © 1982, GIA Publications, Inc.
398 © 1993, GIA Publications, Inc.
399 © 1990, GIA Publications, Inc.
400 © 1984, GIA Publications, Inc.
401 © 1984, GIA Publications, Inc.
402 Descant: © 1979, GIA Publications, Inc.
403 © 1981, 1994, Robert F. O'Connor, SJ, and OCP Publications. P.O. Box 13248, Portland, OR 97213-0248. All rights reserved. Used with permission.
404 © 1995, GIA Publications, Inc.
405 © 1972, 1980, The Benedictine Foundation of the State of Vermont, Inc.
406 Harm.: © 1975, GIA Publications, Inc. Descant: © 1997, GIA Publications, Inc.
407 Descant: © 1991, GIA Publications, Inc.
408 © 2003, GIA Publications, Inc.
409 © 2003, GIA Publications, Inc. Instrument part: © 2004, GIA Publications, Inc.
410 © 1990, 1991, GIA Publications, Inc.
413 Harm.: © 1986, GIA Publications, Inc.
414 © 1984, North American Liturgy Resources. Published by OCP Publications. P.O. Box 13248, Portland, OR 97213-0248. All rights reserved. Used with permission.
415 © 2003, GIA Publications, Inc.
416 Descant: © 1979, GIA Publications, Inc.
417 © 2001, GIA Publications, Inc.
418 © 2001, GIA Publications, Inc.
419 © 1987, GIA Publications, Inc.

420 © 1999, GIA Publications, Inc.

422 © 1981, Les Presses de Taizé, GIA Publications, Inc., agent

423 © 1997, GIA Publications, Inc.

424 Harm.: © 1987, GIA Publications, Inc.

425 © 2001, GIA Publications, Inc.

427 © 2001, GIA Publications, Inc.

429 © 1969, and arr. © 1982, Hope Publishing Co., Carol Stream, IL 60188. All ights reserved. Used by permission.

430 © 1979, Les Presses de Taizé, GIA Publications, Inc., agent

432 © 1997, GIA Publications, Inc.

433 © 1984, Les Presses de Taizé, GIA Publications, Inc., agent

434 © 1988, GIA Publications, Inc.

437 © 1976, Daniel L. Schutte and OCP Publications. P.O. Box 13248, Portland, OR 97213-0248. All rights reserved. Used with permission.

438 Harm.: © 1987, GIA Publications, Inc.

439 Descant: © 1979, GIA Publications, Inc.

440 Harm.: © 1975, Romda Ltd.

441 © 1996, GIA Publications, Inc.

442 Descant: © 1979, GIA Publications, Inc.

443 © 1972, Ediciones Musical PAX, U.S. agent: OCP Publications. Descant: © 988, OCP Publications. P.O. Box 13248, Portland, OR 97213-0248. All rights reserved. Jsed with permission.

447 Tune adapt.:© 1986, GIA Publications, Inc.

449 © 1991, GIA Publications, Inc.

450 © 1993, GIA Publications, Inc.

451 © 1996, Iona Community, GIA Publications, Inc., agent.

452 © 1975, 1979, Robert J. Dufford, SJ and OCP Publications. P.O. Box 13248, ortland, OR 97213-0248. All rights reserved. Used with permission.

453 Tune: © 2003, GIA Publications, Inc.

455 © 1984, Les Presses de Taizé, GIA Publications, Inc. agent

458 © 1975, 1988, Richard Hillert. Descant: © 1976, Concordia Publishing House

462 © 1973, Word of God Music. (Administered by THE COPYRIGHT COMPANY NASHVILLE, TN) All rights reserved. International Copyright Secured. Used by permision.

464 © 2003, GIA Publications, Inc.

465 © 1988, Iona Community, GIA Publications, Inc., agent

466 © 1942, 1970, Hope Publishing Co., Carol Stream, IL 60188. All rights reserved. Jsed by permission.

467 Harm.: from *The English Hymnal,* © Oxford University Press

468 Descant: © 1979, GIA Publications, Inc.

469 Tune: from *The English Hymnal,* © Oxford Univerity Press. Descant: © 1979, GIA Publications, Inc.

471 Tune: from *The English Hymnal,* © Oxford University Press. Descant: © 1992, GIA Publications, Inc.

472 Harm.: © 1986, GIA Publications, Inc. Descant: © 1997, GIA Publications, Inc.

473 © 1997, GIA Publications, Inc.

475 Arr.: © 1975, GIA Publications, Inc.

476 © 1981, 1982, 1987, GIA Publications, Inc.

477 © 1989, GIA Publications, Inc.

478 © 1979, Les Presses de Taizé, GIA Publications, Inc. agent

479 © 1998, Les Presses de Taizé, GIA Publications, Inc., agent

480 © 2002, GIA Publications, Inc.

481 © 1987, GIA Publications, Inc.

482 Arr.: © 2000, GIA Publications, Inc.

484 © 2002, 2003, GIA Publications, Inc.

485 Descant: © 1980, GIA Publications, Inc.

486 Descant: © 1991, GIA Publications, Inc.

487 © 1993, GIA Publications, Inc.

488 Arr.: © 1991, GIA Publications, Inc.

489 Descant: © 1979, GIA Publications, Inc.

490 Harm.: © 1975, GIA Publications, Inc.

492 Harm.: © 1986, GIA Publications, Inc. Descant: © 1997, GIA Publications, Inc.

494 Harm.: © 1986, GIA Publications, Inc. Descant: © 1997, GIA Publications, Inc.

495 © 1980, GIA Publications, Inc.

496 © 1953, Stuart K. Hine. Assigned to Manna Music, Inc., 35255 Brooten Road, acific City, OR 97135. Renewed 1981. All Rights Reserved. Used by Permission. ASCAP)

497 © 1985, GIA Publications, Inc.

498 © 1989, GIA Publications, Inc.

499 © 1991, GIA Publications, Inc.

500 © 1993, World Library Publications, a division of J.S. Paluch Company, Inc. chiller Park, IL 60176. All rights reserved. Used by permission.

501 Arr.: © 1997, Iona Community, GIA Publications, Inc., agent

502 © 1978, John B. Foley, SJ, and OCP Publications. P.O. Box 13248, Portland, OR 7213-0248. All rights reserved. Used with permission.

503 © 2002, GIA Publications, Inc.

504 © 1979, OCP Publications. P.O. Box 13248, Portland, OR 97213-0248. All rights served. Used with permission.

507 © 2001, GIA Publications, Inc.

508 © 1992, GIA Publications, Inc.

509 © 1992, Bernadette Farrell. Published by OCP Publications. P.O. Box 13248, ortland, OR 97213-0248. All rights reserved. Used with permission.

510 © 1998, Les Presses de Taizé, GIA Publications, Inc., agent

511 © 1985, GIA Publications, Inc.

512 © 1993, 2000, Bernadette Farrell. Published by OCP Publications. P.O. Box 3248, Portland, OR 97213-0248. All rights reserved. Used with permission.

513 © 1970, 1975, CELEBRATION (Administered by THE COPYRIGHT COMPA-Y, NASHVILLE, TN) All Rights Reserved. International Copyright Secured. Used By ermission. Acc.: © 1987, GIA Publications, Inc.

514 Harm.: © 1992, Horace Clarence Boyer

515 © 1966, Vernacular Hymns Publishing Co.

516 © 1984, Utryck, Walton Music Corp., agent

517 © 1986, Bernadette Farrell. Published by OCP Publications. P.O. Box 13248, Portland, OR 97213-0248. All rights reserved. Used with permission.

518 Descant: © 1979, GIA Publications, Inc.

520 Descant: © 1979, GIA Publications, Inc.

521 © 2002, GIA Publications, Inc.

522 © 1979, Les Presses de Taizé, GIA Publications, Inc., agent

523 Music: from *The English Hymnal,* © Oxford University Press.

524 © 1999, GIA Publications, Inc.

525 Harm.: © 1986, GIA Publications, Inc.

526 © 1981, Robert J. Dufford SJ, and OCP Publications. P.O. Box 13248, Portland, OR 97213-0248. All rights reserved. Used with permission.

527 Arr.: © 1990, GIA Publications, Inc. Instrument part: © 1996, GIA Publications, Inc.

528 © 1980, Les Presses de Taizé, GIA Publications, Inc., agent

529 © 1984, Utryck, Walton Music Corp., agent.

530 © 1998, Les Presses de Taizé, GIA Publications, Inc., agent

532 Tune: © 1981, Ernest Sands. Acc.: © 1986, Paul Inwood. Published by OCP Publications. P.O. Box 13248, Portland, OR 97213-0248. All rights reserved. Used with permission.

533 © 1998, Les Presses de Taizé, GIA Publications, Inc., agent.

534 © 2002, GIA Publications, Inc.

535 © 1979, Les Presses de Taizé, GIA Publications, Inc., agent.

536 Descant: © 1989, GIA Publications, Inc.

537 © 1976, Daniel L. Schutte and OCP Publications. P.O. Box 13248, Portland, OR 97213-0248. All rights reserved. Used with permission.

538 © 1983, 1987, GIA Publications, Inc.

539 Descant: © 1980, GIA Publications, Inc.

540 © 1978, Damean Music. Distributed by GIA Publications, Inc.

541 © 1973, Jubilate Hymns, Ltd. (Admin. by Hope Publishing Co., Carol Stream, IL 60188). All rights reserved. Used by permission.

542 Harm.: © 1986, GIA Publications, Inc.

543 © 1981, 1993, Robert F. O'Connor, SJ, and OCP Publications. P.O. Box 13248, Portland, OR 97213-0248. All rights reserved. Used with permission.

544 © 1972, Daniel L. Schutte. Published by OCP Publications. P.O. Box 13248, Portland, OR 97213-0248. All rights reserved. Used with permission.

545 Descant: © 1979, GIA Publications, Inc.

546 © 1986, 1991, Les Presses de Taizé, GIA Publications, Inc. agent

548 Descant: © 1979, GIA Publications, Inc.

549 Descant: © 1991, GIA Publications, Inc.

550 © 1982, 1991, Les Presses de Taizé, GIA Publications, Inc., agent

551 Harm.: © The Royal School of Church Music

552 Harm.: © 1986, GIA Publications, Inc.

553 © 1998, GIA Publications, Inc.

554 © 1995, Veritas Publications/Liam Lawton, GIA Publications, Inc., agent

555 © 1953, Doris M. Akers. All rights administered by Unichappell Music, Inc. International Copyright Secured. All rights reserved.

556 © 2000, GIA Publications, Inc.

557 © 2003, GIA Publications, Inc.

558 Arr.: © 1989, Iona Community, GIA Publications, Inc., agent

559 © 1987, GIA Publications, Inc.

560 Harm.: © 1975, Hope Publishing Co., Carol Stream, IL 60188. All rights reserved. Used by permission. Descant: © 1979, GIA Publications, Inc.

561 © 2002, GIA Publications, Inc.

563 © 2003, GIA Publications, Inc.

564 © 1964 (renewed), Appleseed Music, Inc.

565 © 1997, GIA Publications, Inc.

566 © 1982, Les Presses de Taizé, GIA Publications, Inc., agent

568 © 1998, GIA Publications, Inc.

572 © 2003, GIA Publications, Inc.

573 © 1996, World Library Publications, a division of J.S. Paluch Company, Inc. Schiller Park, IL 60176. All rights reserved. Used by permission.

574 © 1998, GIA Publications, Inc

575 © 2003, GIA Publications, Inc.

576 © 1998, Les Presses de Taizé, GIA Publications, Inc., agent

577 Adapt.: © 1997, GIA Publications, Inc.

578 © 1980, GIA Publications, Inc.

579 Descant: © 1979, GIA Publications, Inc.

580 © 1985, Paul Inwood. Published by OCP Publications. P.O. Box 13248, Portland, OR 97213-0248. All rights reserved. Used with permission.

581 © 1989, GIA Publications, Inc.

582 © 1976 by John B. Foley, SJ. Published by OCP Publications. P.O. Box 13248, Portland, OR 97213-0248. All rights reserved. Used with permission.

583 Tune: © 1984, GIA Publications, Inc.

584 © 1993, World Library Publications, a division of J.S. Paluch Company, Inc. Schiller Park, IL 60176. All rights reserved. Used by permission.

585 © 1976, 1979, Daniel L. Schutte and OCP Publications. P.O. Box 13248, Portland, OR 97213-0248. All rights reserved. Used with permission.

586 Acc.: © 1993, GIA Publications, Inc.

587 Harm.: © 1975, GIA Publications, Inc. Descant: © 1997, GIA Publications, Inc.

588 Descant: © 1979, GIA Publications, Inc.

589 © 1994, GIA Publications, Inc.

590 Tune: © 1971, Daniel L. Schutte. Instrument part: © 1992, OCP Publications. Published by OCP Publications. P.O. Box 13248, Portland, OR 97213-0248. All rights reserved. Used with permission.

591 © 1976, John B. Foley, SJ and OCP Publications. P.O. Box 13248, Portland, OR 97213-0248. All rights reserved. Used with permission.

Acknowledgments/*continued*

592 © 1980, Savgos Music, Inc. Administered by Malaco Music Group. P.O. Box 9287, Jackson, MS 39206
593 © 1979, OCP Publications. P.O. Box 13248, Portland, OR 97213-0248. All rights reserved. Used with permission.
594 Descant: © 1980, GIA Publications, Inc.
595 Tune: © 1975, Daniel L. Schutte and OCP Publications. Instrument part: © 1992, Robert J. Dufford, SJ. Published by OCP Publications. P.O. Box 13248, Portland, OR 97213-0248. All rights reserved. Used with permission.
596 © 1975, 1978, Robert J. Dufford, SJ, and OCP Publications. P.O. Box 13248, Portland, OR 97213-0248. All rights reserved. Used with permission.
597 © 1969, 1979, Damean Music. Distributed by GIA Publications, Inc.
598 Harm.: © 1988, GIA Publications, Inc.
599 © 1979, OCP Publications. P.O. Box 13248, Portland, OR 97213-0248. All rights reserved. Used with permission.
600 © 1972, Maranatha! Music and CCCM Music (Administered by THE COPYRIGHT COMPANY, NASHVILLE, TN) All rights reserved. International Copyright Secured. Used by permission. Descant: © 1996, GIA Publications, Inc.
602 Arr.: © 1975, GIA Publications, Inc.
603 Descant: © 1991, GIA Publications, Inc.
605 © 2001, GIA Publications, Inc.
606 © Schaff Music Publishing
607 © 1988, GIA Publications, Inc.
608 © 1987, GIA Publications, Inc.
609 © 2001, GIA Publications, Inc.
610 © 1960, World Library Publications, a division of J.S. Paluch Company, Inc. Schiller Park, IL 60176. All rights reserved. Used by permission.
611 © 1992, 1994, World Library Publications, a division of J.S. Paluch Company, Inc. Schiller Park, IL 60176. All rights reserved. Used by permission.
612 © 1988, GIA Publications, Inc.
614 Harm.: from *Cantate Domino,* © 1980, World Council of Churches
615 © 1995, GIA Publications, Inc.
616 © 1982, GIA Publications, Inc.
617 Acc.: © 2003, GIA Publications, Inc.
618 Acc.: © 2003, GIA Publications, Inc.
619 © 1997, GIA Publications, Inc.
620 © 1993, GIA Publications, Inc.
621 © 2000, GIA Publications, Inc.
622 Descant: © 1979, GIA Publications, Inc.
623 © 1998, GIA Publications, Inc.
624 © 1992, GIA Publications, Inc.
626 © 1986, 1991, Les Presses de Taizé, GIA Publications, Inc., agent
627 © 1991, GIA Publications, Inc.
628 © 1992, GIA Publications, Inc.
630 © 1993, GIA Publications, Inc.
631 Harm.: © The Trustees of Downside Abbey, Bath BA3 4RH, UK. Descant: © 1992, GIA Publications, Inc.
633 © 1989, GIA Publications, Inc.
634 © 1984, Bob Hurd. Harm.: © 1984, OCP Publications. Published by OCP Publications. P.O. Box 13248, Portland, OR 97213-0248. All rights reserved. Used with permission.
636 © 1985, GIA Publications, Inc.
637 © 2001, Les Presses de Taizé, GIA Publications, Inc., agent
638 © 1999, GIA Publications, Inc.
639 Descant: © 1980, GIA Publications, Inc.
640 © 1986, GIA Publications, Inc.
641 Descant: © 1979, GIA Publications, Inc.
643 Harm.: © 1985, GIA Publications, Inc.
644 Descant: © 1979, GIA Publications, Inc.
646 Descant: © 1979, GIA Publications, Inc.
647 © 2000, GIA Publications, Inc.
648 © 2003, Les Presses de Taizé, GIA Publications, Inc., agent
650 Arr.: © 2004, GIA Publications, Inc.
652 © 1986, North American Liturgy Resources. Published by OCP Publications. P.O. Box 13248, Portland, OR 97213-0248. All rights reserved. Used with permission.
654 © 1986, 1988, Bernadette Farrell. Published by OCP Publications. P.O. Box 13248, Portland, OR 97213-0248. All rights reserved. Used with permission.
655 © 1989, Iona Community, GIA Publications, Inc., agent
656 © 1966, 1982, Willard F. Jabusch. Administered by OCP Publications. P.O. Box 13248, Portland, OR 97213-0248. All rights reserved. Used with permission.
657 Arr.: © 1984, Margaret Mealy
658 © 1965, World Library Publications. , a division of J.S. Paluch Company, Inc. Schiller Park, IL 60176. All rights reserved. Used by permission. Descant: © 1996, GIA Publications, Inc.
660 Harm.: © 1938, 1966, J. Fisher and Bro.
661 © 1977, Scripture in Song, division of Integrity Music. (Administered by MARANATHA! MUSIC c/o THE COPYRIGHT COMPANY, NASHVILLE, TN). All rights reserved. International Copyright Secured. Used by permission.
662 © 1981, Damean Music. Distributed by GIA Publications, Inc.
663 © 1981, Daniel L. Schutte and OCP Publications. P.O. Box 13248, Portland, OR 97213-0248. All rights reserved. Used with permission.
665 Arr.: © 1989, The Iona Community, GIA Publications, Inc., agent
666 Descant: © 1991, GIA Publications, Inc.
668 Descant: © 1991, GIA Publications, Inc.
669 © 1990, Bernadette Farrell. Published by OCP Publications. P.O. Box 13248, Portland, OR 97213-0248. All rights reserved. Used with permission.
670 © 2003, GIA Publications, Inc.
671 © 1981, OCP Publications. P.O. Box 13248, Portland, OR 97213-0248. All rights reserved. Used with permission.
674 © 1984, Utryck, Walton Music Corp., agent
675 © 2002, GIA Publications, Inc.
676 © 1993, GIA Publications, Inc.
677 © 1997, GIA Publications, Inc.
678 © 1979, Cesáreo Gabaráin. All rights reserved. Sole U.S. Agent: OCP Publications. P.O. Box 13248, Portland, OR 97213-0248. All rights reserved. Used with permission.
679 Descant: © 1979, GIA Publications, Inc.
680 © 1988, GIA Publications, Inc.
681 © 1978, OCP Publications. P.O. Box 13248, Portland, OR 97213-0248. All right reserved. Used with permission.
682 © 2003, GIA Publications, Inc.
685 © 1986, GIA Publications, Inc.
686 © 1998, GIA Publications, Inc.
687 Arr.: © 1987, Iona Community, GIA Publications, Inc., agent
688 © 2001, GIA Publications, Inc.
689 © 1963, Stainer & Bell, Ltd., London, England. All rights reserved. (Admin. by Hope Publishing Co., Carol Stream, IL 60188). All rights reserved. Used by permission.
690 Harm.: © 1983, Hope Publishing Co., Carol Stream, IL 60188. All rights reserved. Used by permission. Descant: © 1992, GIA Publications, Inc.
691 © 2003, GIA Publications, Inc.
692 © 1995 , The Iona Community, GIA Publications, Inc., agent
693 © 1970, GIA Publications, Inc.
694 © 1983, GIA Publications, Inc.
695 © 1998, GIA Publications, Inc.
696 © 1983, GIA Publications, Inc.
697 © 1987, The Iona Community, GIA Publications, Inc., agent
698 © 1997, GIA Publications, Inc.
699 © 1983, Bernadette Farrell. Published by OCP Publications. P.O. Box 13248, Portland, OR 97213-0248. All rights reserved. Used with permission.
700 © 2003, GIA Publications, Inc.
701 © 1981, Daniel L. Schutte and OCP Publications. P.O. Box 13248, Portland, OR 97213-0248. All rights reserved. Used with permission.
702 © 1990, GIA Publications, Inc.
703 © 1994, GIA Publications, Inc.
704 Descant: © 1979, GIA Publications, Inc.
705 © 2001, GIA Publications, Inc.
706 Harm.: from *The English Hymnal,* © Oxford University Press
707 © 1984, Utryck, Walton Music Corp., agent
708 Arr.: © 1991, Iona Community, GIA Publications, Inc., agent
709 © 1991, GIA Publications, Inc.
710 © 1988, GIA Publications, Inc.
711 Tune: TRO © 1960 (Renewed) 1963 (Renewed) Ludlow Music, Inc., New York, New York. International Copyright Secured. Made in U.S.A. All Rights Reserved Including Public Performance for Profit. Royalties derived from this composition are being contributed to the We Shall Overcome Fund and The Freedom Movement under the Trusteeship of the writers. Inspired bu African American Gospel Singing, members o the Food and Tobacco Workers Union, Charleston, SC, and the southern Civil Rights Movement.Used by permission. Harm.: © 1981 by Abingdon Press
713 © 1995, Hope Publishing Co., Carol Stream, IL 60188. All rights reserved. Used by permission.
714 © 2001, GIA Publications, Inc.
715 © 1992, 1994, GIA Publications, Inc.
716 © 1985, GIA Publications, Inc.
718 © 1985, GIA Publications, Inc.
719 © 2002, GIA Publications, Inc.
720 © 1987, GIA Publications, Inc.
721 © 1967, OCP Publications. P.O. Box 13248, Portland, OR 97213-0248. All rights reserved. Used with permission.
723 Tune: © 1955, 1983, Jan-Lee Music. Used with permission. Acc.: © 1993, GIA Publications, Inc.
724 Acc.: © 1994, GIA Publications, Inc.
725 Acc.: © 1993, GIA Publications, Inc.
726 Descant: © 1979, GIA Publications, Inc.
727 © 1980, 1986, GIA Publications, Inc.
728 © 1966, F.E.L. Publications, assigned to The Lorenz Corp., 1991. All rights reserved. Reproduced by permission of The Lorenz Corp., Dayton, OH.
730 © 1988, GIA Publications, Inc.
731 © 2002, GIA Publications, Inc.
732 Descant: © 1979, GIA Publications, Inc.
733 © 1991, Ken Canedo and Bob Hurd. Published by OCP Publications. P.O. Box 13248, Portland, OR 97213-0248. All rights reserved. Used with permission.
734 © 1994, 1995, Bob Hurd and Pia Moriarty. Published by OCP Publications. P.O. Box 13248, Portland, OR 97213-0248. All rights reserved. Used with permission.
735 © 1999, 2001, GIA Publications, Inc.
736 Acc.: © 1987, GIA Publications, Inc.
737 © 1942, 1970, Hope Publishing Co., Carol Stream, IL 60188. All rights reserved. Used by permission.
738 Arr.: © 2003, GIA Publications, Inc.
739 © 2001, World Library Publications, a division of J.S. Paluch Company, Inc. Schiller Park, IL 60176. All rights reserved. Used by permission.
740 © 1986, North American Liturgy Resources. Published by OCP Publications. P.O. Box 13248, Portland, OR 97213-0248. All rights reserved. Used with permission.
741 © 1994, GIA Publications, Inc.
742 © 1991, Bob Hurd. Published by OCP Publications. P.O. Box 13248, Portland, OR 97213-0248. All rights reserved. Used with permission.
743 © 1982, GIA Publications, Inc.
744 Arr.: © 1994, The Iona Community, GIA Publications, Inc., agent

745 © 1997, World Library Publications, a division of J.S. Paluch Company, Inc. Schiller Park, IL 60176. All rights reserved. Used by permission.
746 Descant: © 1982, GIA Publications, Inc.
747 Arr.: © 1989, Iona Community, GIA Publications, Inc., agent
748 Acc: © 1999, GIA Publications, Inc.
749 © 1993, GIA Publications, Inc.
750 Harm.: © 1985, GIA Publications, Inc. Instrument part: © 1997, GIA Publications, Inc.
752 © 1985, GIA Publications, Inc.
753 © 2003, GIA Publications, Inc.
754 Acc.: © 1999, GIA Publications, Inc.
755 Arr.: © 1998, GIA Publications, Inc.
757 Harm: ©1940, The Church Pension Fund. Used by permission of Church Publishing Incorporated, New York.
758 © 1976, Bud John Songs, Inc./Crouch Music. Administered by EMI Christian Music Publishing. All rights reserved. Reprinted by permission.
759 Descant: © 1992, GIA Publications, Inc.
760 © 2001, GIA Publications, Inc.
762 © 1987, GIA Publications, Inc.
763 © 1998, GIA Publications, Inc.
764 Harm.: © 1975, GIA Publications, Inc. Descant: © 1997, GIA Publications, Inc.
765 © 1995, GIA Publications, Inc.
768 © 1992, Iona Community, GIA Publications, Inc., agent
769 Descant: © 1979, GIA Publications, Inc.
770 Harm.: © 1986, GIA Publications, Inc.
771 Descant: © 1979, GIA Publications, Inc.
772 © 1993, GIA Publications, Inc.
773 © 1990, GIA Publications, Inc.
776 Descant: © 1992, GIA Publications, Inc.
777 Harm.: © 1987, GIA Publications, Inc. Instrument part: © 1997, GIA Publications, Inc.
778 Harm.: © 1986, GIA Publications, Inc. Descant: © 1997, GIA Publications, Inc.
779 © 1975, 1978, 1996, Carey Landry and North American Liturgy Resources. Published by OCP Publications. P.O. Box 13248, Portland, OR 97213-0248. All rights reserved. Used with permission.
781 Arr.: © 1993, 2001, World Library Publications, a division of J.S. Paluch Company, Inc. Schiller Park, IL 60176. All rights reserved. Used by permission.
782 © 2001, GIA Publications, Inc.
783 Descant: © 1980, GIA Publications, Inc.
784 Harm.: © Willis Music Co.
785 © 1974, Hope Publishing Co., Carol Stream, IL 60188. All rights reserved. Used by permission.
786 Arr.: © 1989, The Iona Community, GIA Publications, Inc., agent
788 © 1987, John D. Becker. Published by OCP Publications. P.O. Box 13248, Portland, OR 97213-0248. All rights reserved. Used with permission.
789 © 1998, GIA Publications, Inc.
790 Harm.: from *The English Hymnal,* © Oxford University Press
791 Tune: from *The English Hymnal,* © Oxford University Press. Descant: © 1979, GIA Publications, Inc.
792 © 1993, GIA Publications, Inc.
794 © 1988, GIA Publications, Inc.
795 ©1988, GIA Publications, Inc.
796 © 1984, Les Presses de Taizé, GIA Publications, Inc., agent
797 Acc.: © 1987, GIA Publications, Inc. Descant: © 1997, GIA Publications, Inc.
798 © 1993, GIA Publications, Inc.
799 Harm.: © 1938, 1966, J. Fisher and Bro.
800 Harm.: © The Trustees of Downside Abbey, Bath BA3 4RH, UK. Descant: © 1992, GIA Publications, Inc.
801 © 2002, GIA Publications, Inc.
803 Adapt. and verses: © 2001, GIA Publications, Inc.
804 © 1985, GIA Publications, Inc.
806 © 1984, Les Presses de Taizé, GIA Publications, Inc., agent
807 Arr.: © 1989, GIA Publications, Inc.
808 © 1990, GIA Publications, Inc.
809 Harm.: © 1986, GIA Publications, Inc. Instrument part: © 1997, GIA Publications, Inc.
810 © 2000, GIA Publications, Inc.
811 © 1988, Bob Hurd and Pia Moriarty. Published by OCP Publications. P.O. Box 13248, Portland, OR 97213-0248. All rights reserved. Used with permission.
812 Tune: © 1989, GIA Publications, Inc.
813 ©1978, John B. Foley, SJ, and OCP Publications. P.O. Box 13248, Portland, OR 97213-0248. All rights reserved. Used with permission.
814 © 1994, GIA Publications, Inc.
815 © 2004, GIA Publications, Inc.
816 © 1977, Archdiocese of Philadelphia
817 © 1993, GIA Publications, Inc.
818 Harm.: © 1986, GIA Publications, Inc.
819 © 1997, World Library Publications, a division of J.S. Paluch Company, Inc. Schiller Park, IL 60176. All rights reserved. Used by permission.
820 Arr. and verses: © 1997, GIA Publications, Inc.
821 © 1987, GIA Publications, Inc.
822 © 1966, 1970, 1986, 1993, GIA Publications, Inc.
823 © 2003, GIA Publications, Inc.
824 © 1984, OCP Publications. P.O. Box 13248, Portland, OR 97213-0248. All rights reserved. Used with permission.
825 © 1986, GIA Publications, Inc.
826 Descant: © 1992, GIA Publications, Inc.
827 © 1983, GIA Publications, Inc.
828 © 2001, GIA Publications, Inc.
829 © 1992, World Library Publications, a division of J.S. Paluch Company, Inc. Schiller Park, IL 60176. All rights reserved. Used by permission.
830 © 1987, Ekklesia Music, Inc.
831 © 1997, GIA Publications, Inc.
832 Harm.: © 1968, GIA Publications, Inc.
833 © 1991, GIA Publications, Inc.
835 © 1987, North American Liturgy Resources. Published by OCP Publications. P.O. Box 13248, Portland, OR 97213-0248. All rights reserved. Used with permission.
836 © 1997, GIA Publications, Inc.
837 © 1969, 1979, Damean Music. Distributed by GIA Publications, Inc.
838 © 2003, GIA Publications, Inc.
839 © 1992, GIA Publications, Inc.
841 © 1992, GIA Publications, Inc.
842 © 1993, GIA Publications, Inc.
843 Tune: © 1984, Bob Hurd. Acc. and instrument part: © 1984, OCP Publications. All rights reserved. Published by OCP Publications, P.O. Box 13248, Portland, OR 97213-0248. All rights reserved. Used with permission.
844 © 1988, GIA Publications, Inc.
845 © 1999, GIA Publications, Inc.
846 © 1988, GIA Publications, Inc.
847 © 1938, Unichappell Music, Inc. Copyright Renewed. International Copyright Secured. All Rights Reserved.
848 Harm.: © The Royal School of Church Music. Descant: © 1992, GIA Publications, Inc.
851 © 1978, Damean Music. Distributed by GIA Publications, Inc.
852 © 1978, OCP Publications. P.O. Box 13248, Portland, OR 97213-0248. All rights reserved. Used with permission.
853 Harm.: © 1986, GIA Publications, Inc. Descant: © 1997, GIA Publications, Inc.
854 © 1987, GIA Publications, Inc.
855 © 1993, GIA Publications, Inc.
856 Harm.: © 1983, Hope Publishing Co., Carol Stream, IL 60188. All rights reserved. Used by permission. Descant: © 1992, GIA Publications, Inc.
857 © 1972, 1981, The Benedictine Foundation of the State of Vermont, Inc.
858 Harm.: © 1975, Hope Publishing Co., Carol Stream, IL 60188. All rights reserved. Used by permission. Descant: © 1979, GIA Publications, Inc.
859 © 1989, GIA Publications, Inc.
860 © 1993, GIA Publications, Inc.
862 © 1994, GIA Publications, Inc.
863 © 1990, GIA Publications, Inc.
864 Arr.: © 1989, 1996, Iona Community, GIA Publications, Inc., agent
867 © 1988, GIA Publications, Inc.
868 Arr.: © 1996, The Iona Community, GIA Publications, Inc., agent.
869 © 2002, GIA Publications, Inc.
870 © 1994, GIA Publications, Inc.
871 © 1994, GIA Publications, Inc.
872 Descant: © 1980, GIA Publications, Inc.
874 Descant: © 1992, GIA Publications, Inc.
876 Descant: © 1980, GIA Publications, Inc.
877 Arr.: © 1989, Iona Community, GIA Publications, Inc., agent

1030 Index of Titles

Index of Titles/*continued*